D0924394

INTERPRETING RELIGIOUS EXPERIENCE

Issues in Religious Studies

GENERAL EDITORS

Professor Peter Baelz and Jean Holm

Further titles in the series

THE NATURE OF BELIEF
RELIGIOUS LANGUAGE
THE WORLDS OF SCIENCE AND RELIGION
EVIL, SUFFERING AND RELIGION
INTERPRETING THE BIBLE
THE STUDY OF RELIGIONS
ETHICS AND BELIEF

INTERPRETING RELIGIOUS EXPERIENCE

Peter Donovan

SHELDON PRESS
LONDON

First published in Great Britain in 1979 by
Sheldon Press, Marylebone Road, London NW1 4DU

Copyright © 1979 Peter Donovan

Thanks are due to Humanities Press Inc for per-
mission to quote from *Religion, Philosophy and
Psychical Research* by C. D. Broad.

Printed in Great Britain by
Cox & Wyman Limited, London, Fakenham and Reading

ISBN 0 85969 154 3

CONTENTS

Issues in Religious Studies

GENERAL PREFACE TO THE SERIES

This series of books offers an introduction to some of the central issues involved in religious studies. It aims to be as dispassionate as possible, assuming a serious interest on the part of the reader but neither previous study in the area nor commitment to any religious position. It seeks to combine a basic rigour of thought with a concreteness of approach.

The purpose of each book is to indicate the nature of the issue, the questions raised by it, and the main directions in which thinkers have looked for answers to such questions. It should thus provide a firm foundation on which further study can be built.

The series was designed in the first place to meet the needs of students embarking on courses in religious studies in colleges of education and universities, and of senior pupils following the revised 'A' level syllabuses. However, the books are not in any narrow sense 'text books', and it is hoped that they will be of value to anyone approaching a study of these issues for the first time.

Peter Baelz and Jean Holm

PETER DONOVAN originally qualified in Law and began his studies in philosophy and theology while working as a legal clerk. After taking an MA and BD in New Zealand where he was born and brought up, he was offered an opportunity for research at Oxford into the philosophical aspects of the Doctrine of Providence for which he gained his doctorate. He now teaches religious studies in Massey University, New Zealand, where he lives with his wife and two young children.

INTRODUCTION

EXPERIENCE IS WHAT COUNTS

Religious experience nowadays arouses more public interest than religious doctrine or theology. Unusual types of experiences connected with religions, whether they be mystical states, possession or prophecy, speaking-in-tongues or extra-sensory perception, are described and discussed in an ever-widening range of books, both popular and serious.

For some people, sharing the accounts of extraordinary human happenings is enjoyable in itself, like reading tales of foreign travel or descriptions of lesser-known living creatures. Others look to religious experience to draw lessons from it about human personality and the beliefs and practices of human societies.

But for the people who value religious experience most, it seems to provide first-hand evidence for the reality of the things they believe in, at a time when most other arguments for the truth of religion fail to be convincing. Talking about religion, they would say, is all very well—but it is experience that really counts! As al Ghazālī once put it, we may be told how drunkenness is caused ('by vapours which rise from the stomach and cloud the seat of intelligence'), but to know that is not to *be* drunk.[1] In the end, many believers insist, it is first-hand experience that produces conviction, if anything does.

I had heard of thee by the hearing of the ear,
but now my eye sees thee;
therefore I despise myself,
and repent in dust and ashes.   (Job 42.5–6)

Even those who do not hold religious beliefs may still agree that experience is what really matters. For if it *is* on certain

[1] al Ghazālī (1058–1111), a great Muslim scholar and mystic, used the analogy with drunkenness to show how reason and knowledge cannot grasp what mystical consciousness experiences.

1

experiences that religious beliefs finally rest, then to examine those experiences honestly, from every possible point of view, would seem to be in the interests of all concerned with open inquiry and truth.[2]

This book is intended, then, as much for those who do not think of any of their experiences as religiously significant as for those who do. For the former group, the non-believers, can learn a lot from coming to appreciate the vital part religious beliefs play in the experiences of others. And the latter, the believers, may well need to be encouraged to be fair and honest in appraising their own experiences (and the sometimes enormously confident claims they make on the strength of them).

But of course the distinction between non-believers and believers in religious matters is never as clear in reality as it appears on paper. A great many readers will be half-believers, for whom various experiences (their own or other people's) may well suggest religious meanings, yet never seem conclusive one way or the other. For them, the study of religious experience and its interpretations will at least show why such lack of finality is not very surprising.

It would be very useful to have a few simple rules by which religious experiences and reports of religious experiences could be evaluated. Are they genuine? Do they tell us anything we do not already know? If they do, what sort of information is it? Does it show which beliefs are really true? There are no such simple rules. But there has been much thinking done on the subject by many well-informed and reasonable people. This book is an introduction to some of that thinking.

[2] Selections from the wide range of first-hand reports of religious experiences gathered by the Religious Experience Research Unit (founded in 1969 at Manchester College, Oxford, by Sir Alister Hardy) have recently been published in two volumes: *The Original Vision*, by Edward Robinson, and *A Sense of Presence*, by Timothy Beardsworth (R.E.R.U. 1977). A third volume, *This Time-Bound Ladder*, contains lively discussions of religious experience and the Unit's findings, led by its present director, Edward Robinson.

1

TYPES OF RELIGIOUS EXPERIENCE

Our lives are full of experiences—but just what are they? The word *experience* can include everything we have ever been aware of, our whole experience of living. Or it may refer to certain exceptional occasions, memorable ones or even disastrous ones: the experiences of being married, having children or travelling abroad, for instance, or the experiences of shipwreck, being lost in a strange city or having one's house burgled.

Then again by an experience we may mean not a happening in which we are involved so much as its effect upon us. We learn from experience, and what we learn we call 'our experience'. Thus we can be experienced climbers, artists or yachtsmen: we are good at those things and knowledgeable about them. They are activities in which we can say we have had a lot of experience.

It is useful to start with ordinary examples like these, to remind us how much our experiences involve public things: happenings, goings-on, states of affairs in the world around us, which we ourselves take part in. For the moment *religious* experience is mentioned, there is a common tendency to think only of the private, psychological side of experience, our inner life of awareness and feeling and subjectivity. But as we shall see, there is a good deal more to religious experience than that.

When is an experience a religious one? The answer is, quite simply, when it is the sort of experience which religions are interested in, which they value or consider important. In other words, identifying experiences as religious ones requires us to look at more than just the features of certain kinds of experience. We have to know also about those systems of belief and behaviour which we call religions.

Consider a rather similar question. When does a sound become a musical note? Not when it is an isolated sound, we discover, but when it features in a wider setting, a context of tunes, rhythms, harmonies and so on. An elaborate musical

3

context such as Beethoven's Violin Concerto, for instance, gives enormous significance to certain sounds (the opening drum beats) which on their own are scarcely musical at all. In a similar way, the religiousness of a religious experience hardly begins to appear until it is seen within the rich and elaborate context of a living religion.

Just as we have a workable idea of what various kinds of music are without having to offer a definition (though of course we all know of borderline cases), so we can get along quite well for present purposes with our rough and general idea of what religions are (even though there, too, there are borderline cases).

The usual way of learning to recognize an experience as a religious one is, of course, from the example of other people. Traditions and communities of religious belief have their classic stories and standard cases of experience, which set certain patterns of thought and ways of speaking. As we pick up the ideas and concepts of a religion, its myths and history, its parables and ideals and devotional language, we pick up too a range of standard kinds of experience which are, for that religion, the points at which its words and doctrines come alive for the believer. For some religions, a wide variety of experiences may be important; for others, only a few central experiences are really significant.

Almost every writer on the subject of religious experiences begins by noting the tremendous variety to be considered, and then offers his or her own way of trying to simplify and classify, for easier illustration and discussion. It is useful to know some of the types usually considered, without being too concerned to draw hard and fast boundaries. (Some experiences, inevitably, will have characteristics of several types at once.) In this chapter I shall distinguish four broad classes, which we may call *mystical*, *paranormal*, *charismatic* and *regenerative* types of religious experience.

MYSTICAL EXPERIENCES

In Lecture XVI of his *Varieties of Religious Experience* William James discusses mystical experiences, observing that they are characteristically reported as being *ineffable* (hard to put into words), *noetic* (states of knowledge, not just feelings), *transient* (usually brief, and fading rapidly), and *passive* ('had', rather than 'done'). James's discussion has influenced most later writing on mystical experience and, together with the wide range of

4

examples he offers, should be read by anyone wanting to explore the subject further.[1]

However, as James would himself have insisted, little is gained by trying to arrive at a precise definition of a word like mysticism. People use it in many different ways, depending on their interests and backgrounds. One writer, concerned especially with mysticism in the context of Christian theology, may describe it, for instance, as 'the secret knowledge of God'.[2] Another, with a philosophical interest in the sense of loss of distinctions common in mystical experience, will define it as 'the apprehension of an ultimate non-sensuous unity in all things'.[3] Another, trying to achieve a description free from theoretical assumptions, may treat it as 'primarily consisting in an interior or introvertive quest, culminating in certain interior experiences which are not described in terms of sense-experience or of mental images'.[4]

In each case a different feature (theological knowledge-claim, awareness of metaphysical unity or quest for inner state) is taken as the chief defining characteristic. More commonly still in some recent books is a tendency to call *mystical* almost any sense of transcendence or heightened awareness, achieved voluntarily or involuntarily and felt to be profoundly significant. Such experiences, also known as *peak-experiences, ecstasy* or *timeless moments,* appear from recent surveys to be widely distributed even in modern western society.[5]

Modern thinking about mysticism commonly revolves around one or more of the following questions:

(i) *Is there a single, universal mystical experience appearing under different descriptions in all religions and mystical paths?*

[1] *The Varieties of Religious Experience:* Gifford Lectures at Edinburgh University 1901–2, given by William James, professor of psychology at Harvard. The book is most easily found in the Fontana edn (1970). While James's viewpoint is open to criticisms and his material dated, his approach has still a great deal to teach us, as have the many reports of experiences he records.
[2] David Knowles, *The English Mystical Tradition* (Burns & Oates 1961), p. 2.
[3] Walter T. Stace, *The Teachings of the Mystics* (Mentor 1960), p. 14.
[4] Ninian Smart, 'Interpretation and Mystical Experience', in *Religious Studies,* vol. 1, no. 1, Oct. 1965, p. 75.
[5] See, for instance, Marghanita Laski, *Ecstasy* (Cresset Press 1961); Andrew M. Greeley, *Ecstasy: a Way of Knowing* (Prentice-Hall 1974).

Some writers on mysticism have quite consciously chosen the subject as a means of finding common ground amongst the religions and philosophies of the world. Each faith, each dogmatic system, each set of traditional symbols and imagery, they suggest, has the same underlying origin in human experience, just as sunlight shining through the windows of church, mosque or temple may be coloured in various ways and illuminate very different sacred objects, yet comes itself from the one source.

Aldous Huxley, in *The Perennial Philosophy*,[6] assembles extracts from many mystical writings, arguing that their striking similarity speaks for itself. W. T. Stace's *Mysticism and Philosophy*[7] is a more thorough-going attempt to show that mystical experiences and utterances have a central core, which he takes to be direct apprehension of the pure unity of all things.

> The whole multiplicity of things which comprise the universe are identical with one another and therefore constitute only one thing, a pure unity. The Unity, the One, we shall find, is the central experience and the central concept of all mysticism, of whichever type, although it may be more emphasised or less in different particular cases, and sometimes not even mentioned explicitly.[8]

(ii) *Are there distinct categories of mystical experience, superficially similar, but with quite different implications for the truth of religious beliefs?*

Advocates of this view are commonly Christian scholars concerned to safeguard what they regard as the distinctive character of Christian mysticism, its sense of a union with a transcendent, personal Creator God. Other cases of mystical experience, they insist, where the notion of God is not present in the description given, must be either unrecognized experiences of God, or else essentially different experiences. They may, for instance, be a profound sense of oneness with nature (panenhenic or nature mysticism), or a supposed identity with an impersonal absolute (monistic mysticism, as found for instance in *Advaita Vedānta*, the mystical tradition of classical Hinduism). Advocates of such distinctions, in other words, reject the unifying thesis of writers like Huxley and Stace, holding that it blurs vital distinctions and

[6] 1946. Fontana edn 1958.
[7] Macmillan 1961.
[8] *Ibid.*, p. 66.

does not do justice to the fundamental disagreements between religious traditions.[9]

As we shall see in chapter 2, deciding between these alternative positions is not a matter simply of comparing experiences and drawing a conclusion. It requires also an appreciation of how the way an experience is described and reacted to enters into the quality of the experience itself, making it difficult to compare that which seems to occur under one description, with that under another (e.g. Muhammad's experience, as he supposed, of the Angel Gabriel with Paul's, as he supposed, of the risen Jesus Christ—and both of them with the Buddha's experience of *enlightenment*).

We must be careful, therefore, not to be too quick to draw general conclusions from the similarities *or* from the differences between the utterances of mystics from diverse religious traditions. The need to look well beyond the attempted descriptions of mystical experiences is even clearer in regard to the next question to be considered.

(iii) *Can experiences induced by drugs or brain stimulation, and resembling mystical experiences in quality and effects, be distinguished from the experiences of genuine religious mystics?*

Lively debates have taken place in recent years between advocates and opponents of *induced* mysticism, especially that produced by psychedelic (mind-expanding) drugs.[10]

The issue is complicated by the fact that most ancient religious traditions have a place in them for the use of various techniques and chemical agents. Yoga, fasting, self-torture, breath-control, sensory deprivation and other ways of changing the body-chemistry as part of the quest for religious illumination or release are as old as recorded religion. Sacred foods such as *soma* and other hallucinogenic plants, intoxicants and the inhaling of smoke and incense appear in many legends and traditions, as well as being there to be found, somewhere or other, in even the most respectable living religions. Is there, then, any basis for insisting on a distinction between 'genuine' and 'artificial' mystical experience?

[9] See, for instance, R. C. Zaehner, *Mysticism, Sacred and Profane* (Clarendon Press 1957).
[10] Sparking off the modern debate was Aldous Huxley's *The Doors of Perception* (Chatto and Windus 1954). For further reading see R. C. Zaehner, *Drugs, Mysticism and Make-Believe* (Collins 1972).

The question is one which we shall raise in chapter 6, where we consider whether the discovery of a natural or scientifically-understood cause of an experience rules out the possibility of its having real religious significance.

(iv) *Is mystical experience, as the great religious mystics have supposed, a direct source of knowledge of transcendent realities, independent of reason and the sense-organs?*

James's description of the classic mystical experience as *noetic,* that is, taken to be a state of knowledge and not of mere feeling, marks the most important feature of mysticism for our purposes. Does mystical or any other kind of religious experience really provide access to realities which cannot otherwise be encountered? Is there anything in the claim of typical mystics that at the time of their experience they had a disclosure of profound truth, that they 'saw things as they really are', 'understood all mysteries', and the like?

It is that assumption about mysticism and other religious experience that gives it the authority it has for religious believers, and its importance within the systems of thought in which they attempt to express and formulate their beliefs. Because of their conviction that they have known, seen and understood, they are able to stand up to all kinds of opposition, to remain unmoved by ridicule, and to refuse to be swayed by the apparent counter-evidence to their claims with which they are continually confronted.

To what extent, if at all, can knowledge-claims be based on the having of experiences which produce a great sense of certainty, but which by their very nature are not open to public inspection and test? To that question we shall return in chapters 4 and 5.

PARANORMAL EXPERIENCES

These may be distinguished from mystical experiences in several ways. They are usually less intense and overwhelming. Their occurrence may even go unnoticed (e.g. unconscious telepathy), something almost inconceivable in the case of mystical experience. They lack the characteristic inexpressibility of mysticism. Indeed, they can usually be described in much the same language as the usual experiences of our senses, which makes them sound rather less exalted and profound than mystical experiences.

Their difference from ordinary experiences lies it the fact that, if the descriptions are correct, they suggest that things occur which conflict with the basic physical principles we take for granted in understanding our ordinary perception of the world. The paranormal experiences called telepathy and clairvoyance, for example, seem to involve the transfer of thought or information from one place to another without any of the usual means of communication. The phenomenon called psychokinesis involves the production of effects without the presence of known physical causal connections. Other alleged happenings, such as precognition, materialization and levitation also seem to break the rules by which we understand our usual experiences of time, space and matter.

Though widely recorded in human history, paranormal experiences of those kinds have been far less readily regarded as *religious* phenomena than have cases of mysticism. They have generally been taken as the working of hidden powers of the human mind or soul, perhaps coming finally from religious sources, but not directly related to the experiencing of some divine activity or power. There have, of course, been numerous recorded events in religious traditions which may well be best understood as instances of paranormal powers. The Bible, for instance, contains many possible instances of precognition, action at a distance, and telepathic awareness.[11]

A second group of paranormal phenomena, however, has much greater possible importance for religion. They are the phenomena commonly called *spiritualistic,* and they include apparitions or ghosts, mediumistic communications, and so-called out-of-the-body experiences. These occurrences have commonly been taken as evidence for the reality of a spirit-world and for that reason have a direct bearing on the claims and beliefs of supernaturalistic religions. If mediums, for instance, do have contact with people in a post-mortem state, this fact obviously supports certain religious beliefs about life after death. So too do the accounts of people who, in moments of physical crisis (or sometimes apparently quite at will), feel themselves to be outside their bodies, and having wonderful experiences elsewhere.

[11] Whether paranormal explanations, if we had them, would detract from the religious meaning of prophecies, miracles, etc. is discussed in R. H. Thouless, *Introduction to the Psychology of Religion*, third edn (C.U.P. 1971), ch. 11; and see below, ch. 6. On psychical research and Christianity see E. Garth Moore, *Believe it or Not* (Mowbrays 1977).

How much weight, for religious purposes, can be placed upon these kinds of paranormal experience, depends very much upon the extent to which it is possible to penetrate beneath the verbal report of the experience. People with strong religious beliefs themselves, or living in a culture with an accepted religion, will describe their paranormal experiences in terms drawn from their own personal or cultural beliefs and quite naturally take them to be convincing proof of those beliefs. To point that out, however, is not necessarily to disbelieve the stories of those who have had a striking and paranormal experience; it is merely to set them for discussion in a wider context than is allowed by simply accepting them or rejecting them at face value.

Paradoxically, for those who are impressed by the religious possibilities of psychical phenomena, the more scope given to the former kinds of paranormal power (those involving telepathy, clairvoyance or precognition), the less convincing for religious purposes become the 'spiritualistic' kinds. For more and more of what is taken by a spiritualistic medium to be communications from a world beyond could be accounted for in this-worldly ways, if the medium and others present were credited with various combinations of telepathic powers and perhaps some sort of collective subconscious mind.[12]

Christianity, with its abhorrence of magic and evil spirits, has systematically discouraged the search for paranormal experiences. Indian religions, particularly Buddhism, and indeed most mystical traditions, recognize the possibility of paranormal capacities showing themselves at various stages on the path to enlightenment, though they are widely viewed as likely to be distractions and obstacles rather than religiously beneficial in themselves.

But for all that, well-documented accounts of modern-day paranormal experiences of any kind probably would lend some support to religion. For the experiencing of some paranormal occurrence may well startle someone into taking a greater interest in the possibilities of religious belief. Many young converts to 'Jesus Movement' Christianity in the early 1970s are reported to have been former drug-users seriously shaken by the hallucinatory and paranormal effects of their drug experi-

[12] See 'The Question of Survival', ch. vii of Antony Flew's *New Approach to Psychical Research* (1953), reprinted in Terence Penelhum, ed., *Immortality* (Wadsworth 1973); see also H. H. Price, 'The Problem of Life After Death', *Religious Studies* vol. 3, no. 2, April 1968.

ences. The fact that paranormal powers and capacities seem to have occurred frequently in connection with holy men, founders of religions, saints and charismatics gives the subject further importance in relation to the next class of religious experiences to be considered.

CHARISMATIC EXPERIENCES

All groups and movements have their leaders and heroes, men and women who stand above the crowd of average believers, on account of their superior insight, single-mindedness, holiness of life or strength of personality. The abilities and attainments of such spiritual leaders will usually, in a theistic religion at least, be viewed as *charismata*—that is, as gifts or blessings bestowed on them by God.

The prophets of Israel, for instance, foretold coming disaster, worked miracles or pronounced with authority the judgement of God when 'the Spirit of the Lord' came upon them. In the period between the Testaments a class of Jewish charismatics and holy men continued some features of the prophetic tradition, notably wonder-working, healing, ecstatic praying and exorcism.[13]

Besides these forerunners, the obvious patterns for charismatic experience in Christianity are the earliest apostles and their converts. Our chief information comes from the letters of Paul. In 1 Corinthians he writes concerning 'spiritual gifts':

Now there are varieties of gifts, but the same Spirit; and there are varieties of service, but the same Lord; and there are varieties of working, but it is the same God who inspires them all in every one. To each is given the manifestation of the Spirit for the common good. To one is given through the Spirit the utterance of wisdom, and to another the utterance of knowledge according to the same Spirit, to another faith by the same Spirit, to another gifts of healing by the same Spirit, to another the working of miracles, to another prophecy, to another the ability to distinguish between spirits, to another various kinds of tongues, to another the interpretation of tongues. All these are inspired by one and the same Spirit, who apportions to each one individually as he wills.[14]

[13] See Geza Vermes, *Jesus the Jew* (Collins 1973), and James D. G. Dunn, *Jesus and the Spirit* (SCM Press 1975).
[14] 1 Corinthians 12, 4–11; see also Romans 12.6–8.

11

Besides Paul, the author of Acts provides numerous examples of religious experiences of the charismatic type: the Pentecost phenomena of tongues-speaking and prophecy, revelatory dreams, knowledge of the thoughts of others, healing powers, immunity from snake-bite, and the working of miracles. Such 'signs and wonders' were taken by the early Church as God-given confirmation of the power and truth of the gospel and the authority of the apostles.

Present-day interest within the worldwide Christian community in spiritual gifts taken as signs of life lived 'in the fulness of the Holy Spirit' is popularly known as the charismatic movement.[15] The charismatic, saint, or other outstanding holy person was, of course, a central figure in the medieval Church.[16] And the ideal of the spiritual person, who by example and presence brings blessing to the whole community, has always been alive in Eastern Orthodoxy, as a recent writer explains.

. . . the more intense prayer of certain members of the Church brings them a greater experience of the presence and power of God in the spirit, and makes of them charismatics, whom in Orthodoxy we call 'spiritual men'. These 'spiritual men' feed not only on the Church's liturgical and private prayer, but also on the ascetical and patristic writings which they know sometimes through reading, but more often through the lives of their spiritual fathers, who are actual embodiments of these writings. In this way they learn the doctrine of the purification of the passions and the way of uninterrupted prayer. By these means they make their natures spiritual, so that they become permeable to the Holy Spirit and to the divine light, as Christ was on Mount Tabor. Then they radiate this light, which is also a divine energy, in the form of spirituality, supernatural power, and immense love for men.[17]

The experiences of such holy people are by no means confined to the Judaeo-Christian tradition. Popular Islam has its *walis*, and the *sheiks* and *pirs* of Sufi mystical orders; Hinduism

[15] See W. J. Hollenweger, *The Pentecostals* (SCM Press 1972).

[16] 'Monasticism felt itself from the beginning to be the heir of the charismatic movement in the primitive Church.' From an article on *Charism* in *Encyclopaedia of Theology*, ed. Karl Rahner (Burns & Oates 1975).

[17] *Sobornost*, The Journal of the Fellowship of St Alban and St Sergius, series 7, no. 1, Summer 1975.

its *gurus, sādhus* and *āchāryas. Shamans,* adepts and ecstatics, 'specialists of the sacred' as they are sometimes called, are found in all other religions.[18] The monk, a holy personage, may be regarded as a charismatic also in Buddhism. His spiritual powers are not conceived of as gifts from a god, but are nonetheless graces, blessings of the *Dhamma,* to be used not for selfish ends but in compassionate concern for all sentient beings: 'He who, even as a young Bhikkhu, applies himself to the doctrine of the Buddha, brightens up this world, like the moon when free from clouds' (*Dhammapada XXV*).

Western city life does not bring most of us into contact with any prophets, faith-healers, or even saints. But in societies where such people are widely-known and often encountered, their outstanding qualities and powers carry great weight. In the eyes of their families and neighbours, and amongst their own villagers and countrymen, they are living proof of the reality of powers beyond the everyday world. Being such a person, or even knowing one, can be a most convincing religious experience.

Modern discussions of charismatic experiences often focus on the more spectacular kinds: the powers of healing, visions, speaking-in-tongues, revivals, messiah cults and prophetic movements.[19] But less extraordinary spiritual gifts such as wisdom, grace, courage and peace of mind are every bit as important in the study of religious experience. For these are the qualities most prominent in the lives of outstanding religious figures, and it is those outstanding moments in the lives of ordinary believers which convince them that they are, in fact, in touch with God.

William James spends several lectures on the phenomenon of *saintliness.* Noting certain classic signs of sanctity, such as devoutness, purity, tenderness and charity, asceticism and poverty, he concludes that:

> the greatest saints, the spiritual heroes whom everyone acknowledges . . . are successes from the outset. They show themselves, and there is no question; everyone perceives their strength and stature. Their sense of mystery in things, their passion, their goodness, irradiate about them and enlarge their

[18] See, for instance, Mircea Eliade, *Shamanism* (Routledge & Kegan Paul 1964).
[19] See R. A. Knox, *Enthusiasm* (Clarendon Press 1959); I. M. Lewis, *Ecstatic Religion* (Penguin 1971); W. W. Sargant, *The Mind Possessed* (Heinemann 1973).

outlooks while they soften them. They are like pictures with an atmosphere and a background; and, placed alongside of them, the strong men of this world and no other seem as dry as sticks, as hard and crude as blocks of stone or brickbats.[20]

He observes too, however, that those admirable qualities are particularly liable to what he calls 'corruption by excess'. They are all too easily carried to a degree which destroys their good effects and repels rather than attracts. James lists examples of obsessive and fanatical behaviour resulting from too-zealous piety, remarking in particular on a tendency to aggression and intolerance, on the part of the saintly mind.

The saintly temper is a moral temper, and a moral temper has often to be cruel. It is a partisan temper, and that is cruel. Between his own and Jehovah's enemies a David knows no difference; a Catherine of Siena, panting to stop the warfare among Christians which was the scandal of her epoch, can think of no better method of union among them than a crusade to massacre the Turks; Luther finds no word of protest or regret over the atrocious tortures with which the Anabaptist leaders were put to death; and a Cromwell praises the Lord for delivering his enemies into his hands for 'execution'. Politics come in to all these cases, but piety finds the partnership not quite unnatural. So, when 'freethinkers' tell us that religion and fanaticism are twins, we cannot make an unqualified denial to the charge.[21]

This sobering comment serves to remind us of a point already noted. The *religiousness* of charismatic phenomena and experiences may lie as much in our evaluation of them as in the phenomena themselves. Powerful personal qualities such as contempt, ruthlessness, greed and the ability to stir men to evil and violence can for some people be just as impressive and awe-inspiring as the qualities of saintliness. To choose the latter as divine gifts, while rejecting the former as worldly or demonic, implies standards of judgement not given along with the phenomena themselves. This was rapidly recognized in the early Church. Not every instance of prophecy, tongues or exorcism could be counted as a sign of the power of God; it was necessary

[20] *The Varieties of Religious Experience*, Fontana edn, pp. 363–4.
[21] Ibid., pp. 334–5.

to discern, to test or 'prove the spirits' according to certain standards (notably their conformity to the impression left by Jesus Christ).

Indeed every religion and every sect has its own ideas about which charismatic experiences are valid and which invalid, who are the true prophets and who the false. The experiences are not, after all, self-certifying; a great deal depends on who has them, and what precedes and follows them. So it is by no means clear what conclusions ought to be drawn from the charismatic qualities and experiences of holy men and women, however important a part they play in mankind's religious experience. Certainly the simple conclusions of the charismatics themselves, that they are experiencing direct confirmation of the truth of their beliefs, is no longer so self-evidently convincing once a few comparisons are made and competing claims examined.

To try to label the experiences simply as 'valid' or 'invalid' is not enough. A more comprehensive standpoint must be found. In the meantime charismatic experiences must be noted as something to take seriously, but not uncritically at face-value interpretation.

REGENERATIVE EXPERIENCES

Most of us know someone whose life has been transformed by a religious conversion or some similar experience. The changed lives which impress us most are, we assume, changes for the better, and the terms used in religious circles to refer to the experiences reflect that assumption. They speak of being 'born again', 'renewed', 'revived', 'filled with new life' and so on. The typical features are fresh hope, new meaning and an improved quality of personal life. It is appropriate to call changes of that kind *regenerative* experiences.

Regenerative experiences are usually, in themselves, less extraordinary than paranormal and charismatic experiences (though both the latter may at times accompany regenerative experiences). The observable changes they bring about are not so much physically odd or inexplicable as striking and unexpected in view of our knowledge of the ordinary run of people's lives. The impressiveness is all the greater if there is a dramatic contrast within the life in question, before and after the experience.

In *The Idea of the Holy,* Rudolf Otto portrays as central in

15

all religions an apprehension of awesome holiness, felt as a reality outside the self, which he calls the *numinous*. Arising directly from this experience is another which Otto describes as creature-consciousness: 'It is the emotion of a creature, submerged and overwhelmed by its own nothingness in contrast to that which is supreme above all creatures.'[22] This two-fold experience, holiness and dread, sense of overpowering majesty and feeling of one's own worthlessness, is characteristic of the more dramatic types of conversion and regeneration. We have already noted it in a passage from Job (above, p. 1). Other biblical examples are Isaiah's vision (Isaiah 6.5) and the reaction of disciples to the miracles of Jesus (Luke 5.8–9).

Just as awareness of holiness produces fear, terror and dread at a level far more profound than mere moral guilt or remorse, it also fascinates and attracts, arousing a longing for redemption and salvation. It is the presence of these emotions of numinous wonder and awe that characteristically makes religious conversions more than mere changes in life-style, or the 'turning over of a new leaf'.

Once again William James, in his lectures on Conversion, provides examples for us, reporting many 'crisis conversions' accompanied by extravagant claims and outlandish behaviour. Other examples he gives, while less spectacular, illustrate just as well the newness of life and fresh hope that make this type of experience important for those who undergo it—whether it marks a dramatic turning-point in their lives, or is more subtle and gradual. And indeed it may well be that the most wide-spread of all regenerative experiences in religion is that of ordinary people (i.e. not mystics, charismatics or ecstatics) who through religious belief find their life to be continually filled with meaning and given spiritual value which, so far as they can see, it would otherwise lack.

Other important varieties of regenerative experience are those spoken of as deliverance from evil, salvation, redemption, healing or other occasions where a real improvement in bodily and mental health (either suddenly, as in an escape from death or injury, or more gradually) is taken as a more-than-natural event, and thanks are given to God or some other supernatural being. The experience may be a personal one, or one involving a group

[22] *The Idea of the Holy* (1917), Penguin edn, p. 24.

16

or whole community. The psalms of the Old Testament contain many passages reflecting the experience of both personal and national regeneration, and have no doubt deeply influenced Jewish and Christian piety in this regard.

O give thanks to the Lord, for he is good;
for his steadfast love endures for ever!
Let the redeemed of the Lord say so, whom he has redeemed from trouble
and gathered in from the lands, from the east and from the west,
from the north and from the south.
Some wandered in desert wastes, finding no way to a city to dwell in;
hungry and thirsty, their soul fainted within them.
Then they cried to the Lord in their trouble, and he delivered them from their distress;
he led them by a straight way, till they reached a city to dwell in.
Let them thank the Lord for his steadfast love,
for his wonderful works to the sons of men!
For he satisfies him who is thirsty,
and the hungry he fills with good things.   (Psalm 107.1–9)

As well as regeneration and salvation in the spiritual and physical well-being of people, regeneration in their *moral* life is an experience very prominent in records of religious experience. The sinner, the person wrestling with conscience and plagued by guilt, unable to do what he or she believes to be right and thus powerless and morally defeated, is the classic candidate for conversion and religious rebirth.

H. D. Lewis, in *Our Experience of God*, treats the area of moral experience as particularly important in providing experiences open to religious interpretations and deeply meaningful for the person involved.

It is not merely in the moral life that God speaks—we find Him in other interests and in by-ways where we sometimes least expect Him. But the centrality of ethics for other human concerns, and the difficulty of engaging in any activity without some implicit assessment of worth, make these extensions and intensifications of ethical insights which are due especially to religion of paramount importance in the religious conditioning or toning of human experience and progress.[23]

Natural moral duties take on new force when regarded as the will of God, and the experiences of struggle and achievement (or failure) that accompany them become profoundly religious events for those involved. Thus sin and guilt, conquering evil and finding power for continued improvement in attitudes and behaviour, are central themes in the popular expression of religion.

The meeting of moral needs is, then, an important function of religion, whether such help is received through prayer, worship, the sacraments or in the form of 'grace' or spiritual gifts. Christian hymns, testimonies and confessions are full of reports of regenerative experiences. While these are perhaps most prominent in Protestantism since the Evangelical revivals of the eighteenth century, conversion and grace, salvation and deliverance are characteristic of the lives of believers at all times in the history of the Church.

Other religious traditions, not surprisingly, have their parallels. Thus a convert to Islam tells us:

In the blessed pages of the Holy Qur'ān I found solution to all my problems, satisfaction to all my needs, explication for all my doubts. Allāh attracted me to His light with irresistible strength, and I gladly yielded to Him. Everything seemed clear now, everything made sense to me, and I began to understand myself, the Universe and Allāh. I was bitterly aware that I had been deceived by my dearest teachers, and that their words were only cruel lies, whether they were aware of it or not. My whole world was shattered in one instant; all concepts had to be revised. But the bitterness in my heart was amply superseded by the ineffable joy of having found my Lord at last, and I was filled with love and gratitude to Him. I still humbly praise and bless Him for His Mercy with me; without His help, I would have remained in darkness and stupidity forever.[24]

[23] *Our Experience of God* (1959), Fontana edn, p. 327.
[24] *Islam—Our Choice: Impressions of Eminent Converts to Islam* (1970), p. 37.

18

And the testimony of a follower of Ogamisama, prophetess of a modern Japanese religion, provides us with a deliverance-experience typical of many religions.

> Once my wife and I were going shopping and we were walking by the side of the main road. I was walking ahead and my wife was a few metres behind me. We used to hum 'Na-myo-ho-ren-ge-kyo' [the sacred prayer taught by Ogamisama] at such times. A bus came rushing very fast and people cried out that a lady is killed by the bus. I looked back for my wife because I was afraid that she was crushed by the bus. But I was surprised to see her standing behind me. When I asked my wife what had happened she told me that it was correct that she was just about to go under the front wheels. But some lady lifted her out of danger. She did not know who it was that guarded her and there was no other lady around. We both prayed at the spot and thanked Ogamisama. . . .[25]

What stronger argument is there for most believers to offer for their faith, than an account of some personal regenerative experience, some conversion, healing or deliverance which for them was utterly convincing?

One other type of experience, which may also be classed as regenerative, is that of a sense of compulsion to follow some new course of action, or to take up a different way of life—accompanied by a confident belief that however difficult the task, strength will be found to carry it out. Such an experience is often referred to as a 'call', or as divine commissioning, direction or guidance. Belief in God's grace and providence and involvement in human destiny, not simply accepted as a doctrine, but taken to be operating in living experience, is one of the most basic elements in the sense of God which underlies all theistic religions.

As with charismatic experience, we shall need to distinguish between face-value interpretations and more considered evaluations of regenerative experiences, especially the sense of divine guidance. God or the gods have been taken as guiding people to do an enormous range of things throughout religious history, some of them sublime, some atrocious. Even the person most eager to use phrases like 'I knew it was God's will' or 'The Lord told me to. . . .' from time to time admits to having been

[25] *Ogamisama's World-Wide Newsletter*, Feb. 1972, p. 5.

mistaken in what he or she thought to be the voice of God. Once again, reference to a wider context than the mere experience itself will be called for, however striking or overwhelming may seem a conversion, escape or call at the time.

In this chapter we have surveyed a wide range of types of experience with religious significance. I have not attempted to comment at all on what the experiences really tell us, whether religious conclusions can genuinely be drawn from them, or what has to be said about alternative ways of explaining them. Those are all questions for later chapters. But before we tackle any of those questions, it is necessary to look much more closely at the ways in which the experiences are, as we say, 'put into words'. For it is the process of interpreting, expressing and reporting experiences that will be found to contain most clues to the puzzle of how best to study religious experience and what conclusions to draw from it.

2

INTERPRETATION AND EXPERIENCE

> Jesus prayed: 'Father, glorify thy name'.
>
> Then a voice came from heaven, 'I have glorified it, and I will glorify it again'.
>
> The crowd standing by heard it and said that it had thundered. Others said 'An angel has spoken to him'.
>
> John 12.28–9

Incidents like that are common in religions. An unusual happening occurs, and various interpretations are made, some religious and some not. For those who make a religious interpretation (for Jesus, who hears the voice of God, and some of the crowd who think it was an angel) a religious experience has occurred. For those who simply think it thundered, there is nothing of religious significance about it.

Can people make whatever interpretations they like? What one hears as the voice of God, another thinks is an angel, and the rest take to be thunder. They can't all be right—but does that matter? Is religious experience purely a matter of interpretation?

But what makes something 'purely a matter of interpretation'? Just because interpretation plays a part in experiences, that does not rule out the possibility of being right or wrong about them. Interpretations may be sound ones, after all. They may get at the truth and give genuine information even though, in ambiguous and unclear situations, we often don't know how to decide amongst them.

WHAT IS INTERPRETING?

Interpreting is a kind of *reading*. When we interpret something, we say what it means. Like reading, interpreting is not entirely arbitrary or a matter of private opinion only. For what things

21

mean is not a purely personal matter. The things interpreted and the contexts in which they occur have to be considered, in deciding what interpretations can properly be made of them. Suppose a doctor tells me that certain spots on my skin show that I have measles. The correctness of his interpretation rests on his judgement (gained from experience and backed by his medical knowledge) that there is a reliable correlation between spots of that kind and the state of affairs that is summed up in the expression 'having measles'.

If I interpret your wink as your way of saying 'I know what *you* are thinking', or if I tell from your yawn that you are bored, I am reading your 'body language', voluntary or involuntary, according to certain agreed rules. I am not just making random guesses or having private hunches as to what the wink or yawn means.

Interpreting, then, like reading, is rule-governed. The things interpreted, and the contexts in which they occur, are read according to rules or regularities which to a large extent determine whether or not we are getting our interpreting right. There is thus much more to it than mere personal preference.

But surely, it may be objected, interpretation can also be creative. It is more than simple translation. A good interpretation is the work of an artist or visionary—not a mere follower of rules. It is something *new*.

There certainly is a place for vision and creativity in many forms of interpretation. We speak, for instance, of a pianist's interpretation of a concerto, or a judge's interpretation of the law. And we take them to be contributing something fresh, some discovery of their own, in doing so. Yet the 'discovery' is still something about *the thing interpreted*, and not a purely subjective creation. The pianist thinks the concerto calls for the interpretation he gives it; and the judge believes that his judgement reflects what the law envisages. Both are trying to grasp features of the subject-matter itself, and not merely to express a private whim of their own.

Suppose I sit at the piano with Beethoven's 'Moonlight Sonata' open before me and play 'Three Blind Mice'. Though I may *say* I am offering an interpretation of the Beethoven sonata, my saying so does not make it so. For there is nothing in common between the two works—no shared rule or regularity. There is, of course, a fine line to be drawn between genuine interpretations of the sonata and parodies or popular tunes based on it, or performances so bad that the original is largely lost sight of. And it is just as difficult to draw clear lines between valid and invalid, or genuine and false interpretations of artistic and literary creations. But nonetheless, not just anything can be called an interpretation.

PUTTING EXPERIENCES INTO WORDS

The most usual way of interpreting things (though there are others) is to say in words what they *mean*. Sometimes a mere name or description will do. We hear a thud. 'What's that?' someone asks. 'Just the water-pipes', we say, having heard it often. Or a bell rings. 'Excuse me—someone at the door', we explain to our visitors.

It seems perfectly natural to speak of interpreting our experiences as 'putting them into words'. Yet this is a rather misleading way of speaking, when you come to think of it. For it encourages us to regard our experiences as private happenings taking place amongst our senses and within our minds, happenings for which we choose suitable containers or labels so that they can be brought out into the public world, passed on to others, and reinspected by ourselves from time to time.

But aren't experiences just like that—private to us, and quite distinct from the public world of words and things? Isn't that the very reason why some of them (like the religious ones) are often so hard to talk about at all easily?

We *are* inclined to think that having an experience is one thing, and describing it, putting it into words, is quite another. But in fact our experiences, and the words we put them into, are by no means so distinct and easily separated. Indeed, the words we can use and the interpretations we can make may very much govern the kinds of experience we are able to have. Far from being merely a source of labels and descriptions, our language is the thing that makes many of our experiences possible. Without it we just could not have them.

The point can be made clearer with a few examples. There are some experiences you can have only if you meet certain conditions first. If you can't do algebra or geometry, for instance, you are unlikely to have the experience of coming top of the class in maths. If you can't float, you won't be amongst those who succeed in swimming the English Channel. Non-golfers can't lose a golf tournament. Stay-at-homes won't suffer from travel

23

sickness or jet-lag. Over-thirties don't share teenage emotions. And so on.

In each case, for there to be such-and-such an experience, something more than just an inner feeling or state of mind is necessary. The outer circumstances must first be right, for they help define what the experience itself is, and what significance it has.

Among the relevant outer circumstances, in the case of many of our more complex experiences, one thing is especially important. It is the elaborate network of descriptions and concepts and relations by which we understand the world and our dealings with it. Our grasp of *language*, that is to say, more than anything else, helps us experience and enter into relations with the world of things and people around us. If we are unaware of the discriminations and shades of meaning which words bring to our attention, then the experiences we are capable of having will be limited and lacking in subtlety too.

Non-users of words (babies, for instance, or animals) can obviously have *some* of the feelings which we all have (hunger, pain, sensual pleasure or surprise for instance). But can a baby suffer embarrassment, experience a burden of responsibility, or fear the threat of nuclear war? Does it make sense, to speak of an infant being shocked at vandalism, or worried about the state of the economy? Those emotions and experiences are ruled out for a baby, since it does not yet participate fully enough in the world of human affairs (mapped out by language) in which things like embarrassment, responsibility or worry about the economy come about.

The world of thoughts and words, then, does not merely provide a person with a set of names to be attached to inner experiences which he or she already has but cannot express. It also enormously broadens the range of experiences that are available.

That is especially so with religious experiences. People who lack all familiarity with the language, imagery or world-views of a religious system can hardly be said to be capable of having religious experiences, for they lack the habits of mind and the awareness of significance which make religiously-interpreted experiences possible.

But couldn't they have those experiences all the same—and simply not recognize them, or not be inclined to talk about them in religious ways? We may want to say that. But isn't that rather like suggesting that the non-golfer *can* really have the

24

experience of losing a tournament—only for him it occurs when he (say) misses a bus, or loses his umbrella.

Perhaps losing a tournament *is* something like missing a bus. (We would have to ask the golfer that.) But it could hardly be just the same experience under another description. For its significance in each case is quite different. Totally different consequences follow in the two situations; quite distinct sorts of excuse or explanation are called for; and so on.

In a similar way, the significance an experience has for a religious believer and for a non-believer may be totally different, even if to a casual observer they might seem to be undergoing pretty much the same feelings and emotions. (Would a casual observer be likely to be a reliable guide to such things, we might ask.) The believer may suppose he is being called by God, for instance, while the non-believer may be inclined to think of his experience as a bright idea, or perhaps a twinge of conscience. The interpretations the two parties are in the habit of making are not just something incidental to their experiences. They are very much a part of the situations in which the experiences occur, making the circumstances and the significance (and therefore the experiences themselves) quite different from each other.

ALTERNATIVE INTERPRETATIONS

Yet surely it must be possible for two people to have the same experience and interpret it differently—one in religious terms and the other not. Isn't this just what makes religious experiences so problematic? They always seem open to other interpretations. What some regard as Providence, others call chance. When some speak of divine inspiration, others talk about genius. When some hear an angel speak, the rest merely hear thunder. Aren't we here at the very heart of the problem?

The fact of alternative, competing interpretations of the same facts or experiences does indeed raise a central issue in the discussion of religious experience. How can those who go beyond the non-religious interpretation and make interpretations with religious overtones justify the additional claims and assumptions they make?

We have already seen (in chapter 1) that there is amongst modern writers a dispute about mystical experience and its interpretation. Is there a basic mystical experience underlying

25

all the various interpretations, or are there several irreducible types? We must look further at that question, for it may help us to become clearer about just what it is for two people to have apparently the same experience and yet to interpret it differently.

Consider how the dispute arises. People in various cultures report having impressive experiences which do not have immediately obvious sources or meanings (i.e. are not recognizable instances of impressive experiences associated with food, sex, sport, music, adventure or intellectual activity). When all those and other familiar categories are exhausted, one of the remaining possibilities is a loosely-defined class known as *mystical* experiences. Most cultures have their own ways of accounting for those experiences in religious terms. But when compared across cultures, the reports of those experiences share certain common features; they speak of perceiving reality without using the senses, having exalted states of mind, a sense of timelessness, a loss of self-consciousness; and they use a common imagery of light, beauty, emptiness, bliss, love as ways of describing the 'feel' of the experiences and their supposed significance.

It is therefore often assumed that a basic experience can be isolated, occurring worldwide and throughout history. Individual variations in descriptions of the experience and reactions to it are felt not to be essential to it. They are accounted for by reference to the historical and cultural settings, personal religious beliefs, degree of education and the like, of the people involved. Thus W. T. Stace, in his *Mysticism and Philosophy,* concludes, 'There is reason to suppose that what are basically the same experiences have been differently interpreted by different mystics.'[1]

There is a lot to be said for the view that all mystical experience is essentially the same (at the uninterpreted level). If it were true, that would help clear the air of the claims and counter-claims people so often make, when trying to use mysticism to support their own religious views and to discount those of others. The whole subject of mysticism would be de-mystified and brought down to earth, it might be felt, if the experience involved was found to be one common to all peoples. Even the peak-experiences and ecstatic moments of atheists and humanists would turn out to be as genuinely mystical as any other, differing only in the more modest claims that are made about them.

[1] W. T. Stace, *Mysticism and Philosophy* (Macmillan 1961), p. 18.

But have the advocates of that view too easily assumed that a basic, neutral experience can be found lying behind all mystical experience? Several questions are raised which we can usefully consider.

(i)   IS THE 'COMMON CORE' ONLY AN ILLUSION?

The similar descriptions mystics the world over give of their experiences are often thought to show there is a shared common core. As Stace puts it: 'The language of the Hindus on the one hand and the Christians on the other is so astonishingly similar that they give every appearance of describing exactly the same experience.'[2]

On their own, however, similarities in language can be very misleading. Whether to regard them as astonishing and striking (as is often done) or as superficial and deceptive, we are in no position to judge, without something further to go on. Even if we could be sure that different mystics were describing experiences with similar features, it does not follow that the features in common are the essential features, so far as the significance of the experience goes.

Take a simple example: a group of printed words like 'fry', 'try' and 'pry', or spoken ones like 'some day' and 'Sunday'. Our visual experiences when we read the printed words, and our hearing experiences when we hear the spoken ones, have many common features. Yet what the words or sounds convey is totally different in each case. It is the slight differences, not the common features, that finally determine what each really means. And of course even completely similar sounds or signs can mean quite different things in different circumstances (a red light in traffic lights and in a recording studio, for instance).

(ii)   CAN WE 'STRIP OFF' INTERPRETATIONS TO GET TO A NEUTRAL EXPERIENCE?

But surely a neutral description is possible, if enough care is taken—a description of the *feel* of an experience itself, without interpretations reflecting any particular point or view of belief-system. Isn't this the best way to get at what is really taking place?

There are, however, serious difficulties in the idea of seeking

[2] *Ibid.*, p. 36.

a neutral core to mystical experiences by stripping off their theory-laden interpretations and concentrating only on their felt properties. The first question to be asked is, why should it be supposed that the less the amount of interpretation, the nearer we get to the essential meaning of an experience, while the greater the amount of interpretation the further we get from the true meaning? It is, after all, just as possible to miss the genuine significance of an experience through under-interpretation as it is through over-interpretation.

That is clearly so in the case of our knowledge of human actions and intentions. For one of the commonest ways of mis-understanding someone is to make too simple an interpretation of his words or behaviour. (For instance, when I miss the point of a reassuring nudge from my wife, and think she is just being a bit clumsy with her elbows!)

And it is true also in the case of scientific knowledge (of physical, chemical, geological and other facts). In none of those cases is an uninterpreted, neutral experience on its own a source of objective information at all. For it is only when quite elaborate theoretical interpretations (involving concepts of space and time, molecular structure, mass and gravity and the like) are added to our simpler experiences of the physical world that anything approaching knowledge or understanding of its total significance begins to develop.

It may be that mystical experiences, too, can only be properly appreciated by reference to the interpretative belief-system (and in fact the mind and behaviour as a whole) of the person whose experiences they are. If so, then trying to strip off interpretations in search of a neutral, core experience could be quite the wrong approach to take.

(iii) IS AN UNINTERPRETED EXPERIENCE EVEN A POSSIBILITY?

Mystical experiences, or any other kinds of experience for that matter, are experiences which people have. Since it is of the nature of an experience to be *someone's* experience, the idea of a neutral, uninterpreted experience is a purely artificial one. There can never be such a thing in fact, for people are never free from theories and belief-systems.

It is all very well, then, to speak about 'comparing people's experiences at the uninterpreted level'—at the level of a des-cription of pure 'feel', if you like. For even the feel will be a property of an experience which, for the person who had it, *was* interpreted in some way or other (i.e. was taken to be one sort of experience rather than another). So though we may tell the experiencer to 'bracket out' the interpretation and just describe the feel, it is still the feel of *that* experience we are getting, the one that was experienced under that (bracketed out) interpretation.

In fact it becomes very difficult to say how experiences could be individuated (marked off from one another) at all, at some uninterpreted level. Someone once defined a tennis net as 'holes joined together by string'. The search for completely uninterpreted experiences is a little like the search for a 'pure' hole, one without any surroundings at all. What would make such a pure hole the hole it is, rather than some other pure hole? Similarly, no means for identifying or individuating experiences seem to remain, once all interpretations (actual and possible) are left out of the picture, for it is largely they which make an experience the experience it is.

(iv)   WHAT ABOUT RE-INTERPRETATIONS?

Yet there is no doubt that we *can* be undecided about how to interpret an experience which we have unquestionably had. Doesn't this show that an experience is *there*, before interpretation, and therefore that there can be such a thing as a neutral, pure experience?

But even if we are undecided about what interpretation finally to adopt, the fact that we have *recognized* an experience at all means inevitably that some interpreting has gone on. Can experiences be thought about at all (even for the purpose of trying to give them a neutral description) except under some interpretation or other, however minimal or provisional? For the range of *possibilities* we are aware of and prepared to consider will already have shaped for us any experience of which we become conscious. Experiences never occur in a vacuum, to a completely neutral experiencer. There are no such people.

But what is to be said of the many experiences about which we change our minds? 'I thought she was waving to me, but then I realized that she was trying to catch a butterfly.' 'I took his remarks as a compliment, but when I thought about them for a while I saw that he had insulted me.' Do not cases like those show that there must be an underlying experience already

29

there, to which different interpretations come to be applied?

But those cases are not examples of totally bare experiences, to which various interpretations are later attached, one after another, until the right one is found. On the contrary, they are overloaded with interpretations, from the very beginning.

An ambiguous word (like *bank*, or *tear*) is not something neutral, something that is meaningless until we choose a suitable meaning for it. It is already too rich in possible meanings, and we have to consider its context, speaker, etc., in an effort to narrow down that meaningfulness. Ambiguous experiences (ones we may change our minds about), even more than straightforward ones, require of us a prior knowledge of available interpretations. It will not help us at all, in deciding about their meanings, to think of them as purely neutral or to concentrate on their feel or sound alone.

What has happened, then, to the suggestion that the way to study mystical experience is to look for a bare, uninterpreted experience to begin with—one that is common to many mystics, however different their religious beliefs and interpretations? Completely uninterpreted experiences seem to be harder to find than we thought. And if that is true of mystical experiences, it is even more apparent in the case of non-mystical kinds of religious experience (e.g. conversion, saintliness, prophetic inspiration or the ability to heal).

For as we noted in chapter 1, the *feeling* of an experience is often not a particularly central feature of it at all. Think again of such experiences as being shipwrecked, losing a golf tournament, suffering jet-lag or being worried about the economy. Various feelings no doubt go with all those. But is it by their *feel* that we learn to identify those experiences, and talk about them? Doesn't it involve a much larger context, made up of situations and events and relationships out there in the world, and not just confined to our inner states?

The question whether two people are having the same experience and interpreting it differently, then, turns out to be not a straightforward question at all. What makes it so difficult is the fact that experiences are not bare objects, able to be detached from their living contexts and compared with one another independently of the way they are experienced and interpreted by particular people in particular situations.

But can't we do *anything* about the problem, in that case? Surely there must be a way of deciding who is right and who is wrong, who is over-interpreting and who is not, in those ambiguous and puzzling situations so common in religion (cases like the voice of God or thunderclap, providence or chance, inspiration or genius, answered prayer or stroke of luck).

The temptation in such cases is to *impose* an interpretation, in an effort to settle the question. It is easy to smuggle into the discussion an assumption that we, the onlookers, know the rights and wrongs of a dispute, even if the parties to it don't. Thus one writer has concluded: 'Religious emotions are simply aesthetic ones which their owners have misinterpreted.'[3] That may appear to dispose of the question without further ado. But how could we ever know if that view is a correct one? To assume that religious experiences really are just the same as certain non-religious ones (despite the quite different interpretations those who have them make) may be just to settle the dispute by begging the very question at issue.

Was Jesus mistaken, in thinking thunder to be a voice from God? Or did the crowd mistake a voice from God for thunder? These are not simply questions about two alternative interpretations of the same thing (a certain noisy experience which all parties shared). To assume that is to assume we know, somehow or other, that a voice from God and thunder would sound much the same even to those who knew the difference. But we don't know that at all. Someone (Jesus perhaps) who knew how to recognize genuine voices from God might insist that they were quite unlike thunder.

Similarly, those who have genuine religious experiences (if they do) may at times be quite capable of distinguishing them from the alternative, non-religious experiences which the non-religious assume are all that is *really* going on. Just as a person trained to detect forged bank-notes might say that to him a poor forgery looked quite unlike the real thing, even though it might easily fool the rest of us; and that anyone for whom the forged note and a genuine one did look just the same simply wasn't competent to be making the comparison.

There are solid reasons then for resisting the suggestion that it is merely the interpretations supplied by religious believers, and not the experiences themselves, that make their religious experiences significantly different. That might indeed be someone's reasoned conclusion after a thorough study of the subject. But it

[3] Brigid Brophy in *The Humanist Outlook*, ed. A. J. Ayer (Pemberton 1968), p. 195.

ought not to be a starting-off point in the discussion, unwittingly adopted through failing to see just how much lies hidden in the phrase 'alternative interpretations of the same experience'.[4]

INTERPRETING THE INEXPRESSIBLE

Suppose interpreting is a kind of reading or putting into words what something is thought to mean. What if there are things which *can't* be put into words? Some people, including many experts in religion, have thought that we cannot put into words the most important religious experiences of all. They tell us that it is a mistake to try to express the inexpressible. If such experiences are to be interpreted at all, they say, that can be done only by silence, or by other wordless responses such as awe, obedience or repentance.

The commonest occasion for saying 'words fail me' is when an emotion or experience seems too intense for us to put into words. Such a complaint about the inadequacy of words is not, of course, found only in religious contexts. Why can't some experiences be put into words? Obviously words are not *the same as* experiences, and so cannot completely replace them. I can mention the taste of coffee and perhaps bring it to your mind (by saying words like 'the taste of coffee'). Yet my words are not much of a substitute for coffee, if you are thirsty. The words which express and interpret an experience may fall a long way short of actually bringing the experience itself about.

However, it would often be hard to have certain experiences at all, if we were unable to use words to specify just what it was we wanted. (How could we plan meals, follow directions, or share in the thoughts of others, without words or some alternative form of communication?) Even though words do fall short of experiences, our very ability to say (in words) that they do often goes a long way towards expressing what we want to convey. Thus we may use ideas like speechlessness, running out of words, being struck dumb, etc., as devices to emphasize our meaning. *Inexpressible* joy, *unutterable* pain, grief *beyond words,* are all capable of being spoken about. But because the experiences or emotions are far more intense than our usual joy, pain or grief the familiar words scarcely begin to meet the situation.

[4] For a fuller discussion of 'seeing the same thing', see N. R. Hanson, *Patterns of Discovery* (Cambridge 1958), chapter 1.

It is perfectly reasonable to admit that there are things we do not know (what causes cancer, for instance, or how the universe began). Also that there are things we have some appreciation of but cannot yet put into plain language. In a sense, such things are 'unutterable' or 'ineffable' (i.e., cannot be put into words) for us at present. At the growing edge of human knowledge we constantly have to find new terms, clearer and better concepts, for expressing and organizing what we are discovering. We are also constantly having to refine and revise our existing ways of stating what we know.

It is something like that which lies behind the appeal to ineffability made by mystics and religious philosophers. For it is characteristic of mystical and religious thinking to believe that what is encountered in religious experience, God or absolute reality, Brahman or the Void, is *ultimate*. Human thought, which is non-ultimate, cannot set bounds to an ultimate reality. No concepts can be finally applied to it, since the possibility that they will need revising or replacing remains permanently open. Therefore all that is said is said provisionally, and is at best only partially the truth of the matter. The traditional Christian term for this idea has been the doctrine of God's *incomprehensibility*.

Of course, if the source of religious experiences or mystical consciousness were *totally* indescribable, there would be no reason for supposing it to be of an object of worship, a giver of spiritual enrichment, or a treasure to be valued above all else. Why indeed call it 'God', 'Brahman', 'Nirvāna' or any other name with specifically religious associations? It would be at most an unknown X.

When it is said that God (or some other ultimate reality) is inexpressible, this must be taken to mean not that one can say absolutely nothing about God, but rather that one can say nothing *absolutely* about God. For God would not be an ultimate reality if any words or descriptions could fully comprehend or be 'the last word' on the subject.

How inexpressible then is religious experience in general? Religious experiences have sometimes left believers breathless with wonder or dumb with ecstasy. But none of those occasions forces us to conclude that human language is entirely unsuitable for expressing and interpreting religious experience. Quite the opposite is true. Religions are rich in words, with their prayers, poetry, myths and hymns, shouts of praise, confessions of faith,

33

revelations and prophecies, chants and mantras, and countless sermons and theological writings. The impressive thing, when we look at religion, seems to be not the inadequacies of language, but the extent to which human language is fundamental, for interpreting religiously significant experiences as well as for formulating and expressing belief.

The inexpressible, unspeakable side of religious experience is not just a lack of adequate words, but a meaningful silence which gains its significance from the context of interpreted experiences, beliefs and expectations which surround it. And to grasp those experiences and enable them to contribute to the background of beliefs, words are quite indispensable. It is only because of what we *can* say then that what we can't express about religious experience is able to be religiously important.

INTERPRETATIONS AND THEOLOGIES

Theologies arise through the systematizing of the words and concepts, the names and the analogies, used in religious interpretations of experience. They are attempts to gather together and account for the meanings found in the experiences and phenomena basic to a particular religious tradition.[5]

Theological thinking is a way of exploring life. Traditional theologies indicate where significance has been found, and suggest why it is there to be found. The words, concepts, metaphors and parables in a religious tradition, if they do in fact help believers to find God, eternal life, Nirvāna or some other spiritual goal, do so by contributing to their ability to find religious meaning within the events and experiences of life.

Have you ever heard the lay-preacher who tells his congregation that he 'doesn't know any theology, but he does know the Lord'? Despite his denial, of course, he does know a good deal of theology. And if he didn't, he just wouldn't know what he was talking about when he spoke of 'knowing the Lord'. Even what may seem like the simplest interpretation of a religious experience in Christianity—for instance, what a believer calls 'knowing the Lord'—takes for granted a whole lot of theology.

[5] It may quite rightly be objected that there are religious systems such as Theravāda Buddhism and Taoism which cannot have *theologies* since they lack the idea of a supreme god. The solution is not to limit the discussion to theistic religions, but to widen the definition of *theology* to cover the theoretical system in any religion by which people interpret and reflect upon their experiences.

For it is a theology or belief-system which gives the title *Lord* a meaning, identifies it with a particular person in history, implies that that person is still able to be involved, in some sense, in a believer's life. It is within a theological belief-system that certain kinds of experience, rather than others, are taken to be reliable signs of the presence or activity of Christ. All that theoretical background is not found in the experience itself but is brought to it by way of interpretation, making it the experience it is.

Even the simplest interpretation of an experience in religious terms, then, is heavily theory-laden (or theology-laden, if you like). It takes for granted many complex theological claims as correct, even if it makes no attempt at all to establish that they *are* correct. It thus becomes much more difficult than appears at first glance, to try to justify religious beliefs by appealing directly to certain experiences. Of course, for the person who has the experience and interprets it without question by a particular theological description, it will seem convincing and conclusive. But the open-minded student of religions, aware of the vast range of possible interpretations and conflicting theologies available, will want to ask what led the experiencer to describe his experience as, for instance, an encounter with the risen Christ and not, perhaps, with some other deity; or an imagined human presence; or simply an exalted state of mind with no particular religious meaning at all. In other words, what reason is there for assuming that the experiencer has got his interpretation right?

The varieties of experiences open to religious interpretations appear to be endless. That does not mean that one interpretation can be no better or nearer the truth than another. But it does make it obvious that the truth or falsity of an interpretation is not to be found by looking merely at the experience involved. It is necessary as well to examine the whole theological system in terms of which the interpretation of that experience is made.

So religious belief-systems and human experiences need each other, and interpretations are what bring them together. When belief-systems seem to be matched by experiences, so that the latter can be interpreted with the help of the former, is there any basis for an argument that the experiences help establish the *truth* of those beliefs? That question we shall begin to consider in the next chapter.

3

ARGUING FROM EXPERIENCE

Do religious experiences really prove anything, one way or the other, about the truth of religions? Millions of people have thought that they do. They have taken them to be reliable guides to the indescribable state of Nirvāna, overwhelmingly convincing encounters with the risen Christ, or infallible confirmations of the words of some sacred scripture or inspired prophet. The enormous number of different claims based on experiences, however, can easily put thinking people off the subject altogether (especially when they remember the countless religions of other times and places about which next to nothing is known). It is only natural to feel 'they can't all be right', and to conclude that perhaps they are all mistaken.

In chapter 2 we saw that interpretation can be a rational process. It is not necessarily arbitrary or utterly subjective. But that merely raises the *possibility* that religious interpreting is a way of getting at the truth. It is quite another thing to show that genuine knowledge about the objects of religious beliefs can really be gained from religious experience. The next three chapters will look, stage by stage, at that larger question, and some of the ways in which it has been approached in recent thought.

Why should people believe in God? Because God is real and can be experienced like any other reality, religions tell us. Arguments for the existence of God based on the fact of religious experience take many forms. The one chosen for discussion here comes from Professor C. D. Broad's essay 'Arguments for the Existence of God'.[1] We shall look also at some more recent discussions, along similar lines.

[1] C. D. Broad, 'Arguments for the Existence of God', in *Religion, Philosophy and Psychical Research: Selected Essays* (1953), reprinted Humanities Press 1969, pp. 175–201. As Broad's discussion is a model of philosophical writing, I have reproduced the central points in Broad's own words. It is worth taking the time to read the quotations themselves carefully.

The main premise of the argument is that enormous numbers of people have had religious experiences. But haven't enormous numbers of people *not* had religious experiences, as well? Broad does not for a moment deny that however widespread religious experience is, or has been in the past, it is by no means *universally* found or uniformly appreciated.

> Some people seem to be almost wholly devoid of any specifically religious experience; and among those who have it the differences of kind and degree are enormous. Founders of religions and saints, e.g., often claim to have been in direct contact with God, to have seen and spoken with Him, and so on. An ordinary religious man would certainly not make such a claim, though he might say that he had had experiences which assured him of the existence and presence of God.[2]

ANALOGY WITH MUSICAL EXPERIENCE

Is a lack of capacity for religious experience something like the lack of an ear for music? Broad reminds us that differences of degree in appreciation of music are great, and that 'those who have not much gift for music have to take the statements of accomplished musicians very largely on trust'. Perhaps the analogy with musical experience shows us that wide differences, with regard to religious experience, are only to be expected.

> Let us, then, compare tone-deaf persons to those who have no recognizable religious experience at all; the ordinary followers of a religion to men who have some taste for music but can neither appreciate the more difficult kinds nor compose; highly religious men and saints to persons with an exceptionally fine ear for music who may yet be unable to compose it; and the founders of religions to great musical composers, such as Bach and Beethoven.[3]

The analogy is a tempting one, at least for the arguer for religion. It enables him to explain why his more sceptical friends never seem to sense the awful divine realities, experience the depths of guilt, or realize the joys of forgiveness that mean so much to

[2] Broad, *op. cit.*, p. 190.
[3] *Ibid.*

him. They are spiritually tone-deaf, and therefore insensitive to religious experience. After all, do not the Scriptures say:

This people's heart has grown dull,
and their ears are heavy of hearing,
and their eyes they have closed,
lest they should perceive with their eyes,
and hear with their ears,
and understand with their heart,
and turn for me to heal them.

(Matthew 13.15, quoting Isaiah 6.9)

Yet the analogy between musical insensitivity and lack of capacity for experiencing things religiously needs to be carefully handled by the defender of religion. For of course there is one very important difference between music and religion, so far as experiencing goes. Musical experience does not claim to be a means of knowledge about the ultimate nature of reality, while religious experience does. As Professor Broad puts it,

Granted that religious experience exists, that is has such-and-such a history and conditions, that it seems vitally important to those who have it, and that it produces all kinds of effects which would not otherwise happen, is it *veridical*? Are the claims to knowledge or well-founded belief about the nature of reality, which are an integral part of the experience, *true or probable*?[4]

There is no question about musical experience being veridical (i.e. truthful about its object, valid in its portrayal of reality) since it is not taken as being experience of anything beyond itself. On the other hand, religious experience as traditionally viewed is taken to be a source of information, of a special kind, about the things beyond ordinary natural life with which religions are especially concerned.

But is it essential to insist on that traditional view of religion as the only possible one? In his book *Religious Experience*, T. R. Miles has argued that the significance and validity of religious experience remain even if it is not regarded as a source of information about a supernatural God or some state of affairs 'beyond the natural world'.

[4] *Ibid.*, p. 191.

For Miles, the question is not whether religious experience does or does not give information about a supernatural God. For he considers (on philosophical grounds) that we cannot nowadays make sense of the idea of a transcendent God existing 'beyond the world', who answers prayers, guides people, or reveals himself in human experience. Such ideas of God, he suggests, are really *parables* by which people have attempted to answer and respond to certain cosmic questions (Who am I? What is man? What do life and death mean?).

It is those questions themselves, rather than the traditional answers to them, that are the essence of religion. And for Miles, religious experiences are the experiences a person has 'when he tries to come to terms with cosmic issues'. As with musical experiences, there is no need for religious experiences to be evidence for something beyond themselves. The experiences are what they are. They are experiences of many kinds (obligations, solitude, kindness, beauty, wonder) which come as answers to a person's cosmic questions, as he tries to live life according to the way of life commended in one or other of the religions.

A traditionally interpreted experience, Miles explains, needs to be reinterpreted as follows:

If people claim to have experienced 'the presence of the risen Christ', this is not a literal reference to the actual Jesus Christ who genuinely died somewhere around the year A.D. 29. In this case the demand that people should allow the spirit of Christ to work in their hearts carries many practical consequences; and it can fairly be argued that recognition of the compelling nature of this demand is more important than acceptance of the mythology in which it is expressed. In my own view the mythology can be dispensed with as long as the cosmic significance of the demand is fully recognized.[5]

Miles admits that answers to cosmic questions 'do not occur *in vacuo*; they arise in the context of a particular religious tradition with its own particular practices, symbols and world-picture'.[6] But the function of the theology, he considers, is not to provide a set of true beliefs, but to offer helpful parables which may evoke the appropriate experiences even though not

[5] T. R. Miles, *Religious Experience* (Macmillan 1972), p. 44.
[6] *Ibid.*, p. 35.

themselves giving a description of any supernatural reality or state of affairs.

People certainly can, if they choose, 'dispense with the mythology' (the theological belief-system) and take religious beliefs to be poetic, non-descriptive parables. They can still find much to appreciate in the experiences of life which those parables bring to their attention. There is no need for them to commit themselves to any theological theories or beliefs beyond the experiences themselves.

There *are* many philosophical difficulties in trying to talk about a supernatural, transcendent God who acts within the world and in human affairs. Those who agree with Miles that those difficulties are too great, and therefore that God as traditionally thought of is an unintelligible idea, could well adopt the view of religious experience which he recommends. Understood in that way, religious experience would indeed be similar to musical experience: a way of appreciating things which justifies itself, without reference to anything beyond.

But religious experiences of the Miles type do differ in an important way from the more usual ones. Consider two people, John and George. John sings 'A mighty fortress is our God' and believes that God actually does protect people, in providential and even miraculous ways, from time to time. John thus faces life optimistically, with confidence that he is safe, in some profound and ultimate way. George, who doesn't think there is a God who acts in the world or in people's lives, also finds 'A mighty fortress is our God' to be a stirring hymn which helps *him* to face life confidently and optimistically.

With the idea of God as an all-powerful, protecting force in mind, then, both John and George find religious overtones in the various experiences, good and bad, which come their way. But John finds something more than just religious meaning in his experiences—some of them he takes to be *evidence* for the truth of his beliefs about God. His religious experiences (along with similar ones other people have) seem to give him good reasons for his optimism and his feelings of ultimate security.

For George, on the other hand, his optimistic view of life (like an appreciation of music) is something he gives no reasons for. He is fortunate to have it, perhaps, and it certainly does make his life richer and happier, but it is essentially non-rational all the same. Religious experience, for George, is something to be appreciated and enjoyed, not reasoned over or argued about.

Even in the case of musical appreciation, of course, it does make some sense to ask some questions and to do some reasoning. For where does music come from, and why is it the way it is? Miles reproduces some bars from Mozart's 'Marriage of Figaro' and Beethoven's fifth symphony by way of example. Of each he says, 'The music here speaks for itself; it is not "evidence" for something else.' But though for the ordinary music-lover that may be so, it is also true that (for music scholars at least) excerpts from the works of a composer can tell a good deal about his creative abilities, the forms on which he drew, and the ideas and intentions he had.

In other words, there *are* questions to be asked about music, even though for its popular enjoyment and appreciation they may not be particularly important. Similarly, then, in the case of religious experiences, while it may be true that the experiences are what they are regardless of theoretical questions about their origins and wider significance, those questions can still make sense and be worth asking. The amount of attention they have received throughout history, and the extent to which they still figure in lively theological and philosophical debate, suggest that the meaningfulness and relevance of concepts like that of a transcendent, active God is much more of an open question than Miles takes it to be.[7]

The analogy between religious experience and musical experience is a suggestive one. It may be useful for reminding us of a form of experience about which theoretical questions are quite out of place. On the other hand, it can also suggest that even with apparently quite uninformative experiences (like musical ones) there are questions to be asked about what lies behind the experience, its cause or source.

In either case, the fact that there are people who do not have the necessary experiences does not in itself count against the genuineness of the experiences of those who do. But it is a fact to be taken account of and not lightly dismissed or conveniently ignored.

Broad warns us that 'any theories about religious experience constructed by persons who have little or none of their own

[7] For a discussion of other views of religion similar to Professor Miles', see chapter 3 of my *Religious Language* (Sheldon 1976), in the Issues in Religious Studies series.

41

should be regarded with grave suspicion'. But at the same time it is also true that the possession of a great capacity for musical, or religious, experience is no guarantee of sound judgement or critical insight.

A man may be a saint or a magnificent musician and yet have very little common sense, very little power of accurate introspection or of seeing causal connections, and scarcely any capacity for logical criticism. He may be almost as ignorant about other aspects of reality as the non-musical or non-religious man is about music or religious experience. If such a man starts to theorize about music or religion, his theories may be quite as absurd, though in a different way, as those made by persons who are devoid of musical or religious experiences.[8]

A rich store of first-hand religious experiences may give a believer great confidence and make him an outstanding figure in the eyes of those who think as he does. But it does not on its own make him an expert about religion, any more than having a good appetite makes one an expert on nutrition.

ANALOGY WITH SENSE-PERCEPTION

Arguments from religious experience often go like this:
Q. How do we come to have our everyday beliefs about the real, material world?
A. We perceive the world through our sense-experiences (sight, touch, etc.). And we confirm our perceptions by finding that a majority of other people seem to share them.
Q. Well, then, when large numbers of people seem to share similar religious experiences, can you deny that they may be perceiving the kinds of reality of which religions teach?
The arguments, in other words, try to show that there is an analogy between sense-perception and religious perception—with experience playing a similar role in both cases.
No one usually doubts that sense-experience, when operating under normal conditions, gives reliable knowledge of a real world beyond itself. We know our sense-experiences are reliable when they have the support of the agreement of others, and when they meet certain tests (when the information they seem

[8] Broad, *op. cit.*, pp. 192–3.

to give us about the world is coherent, consistent with our other knowledge, repeatable, and coercive—that is, hard to ignore).

But so too with religious experience, it is argued. While it does not meet the same tests as sense experience (after all, its supposed object is very different from the objects of sense-perception), reliable criteria and recognized tests are there to be found in the religious tradition appropriate to the object experienced.

In fact, keeping us aware of the tests for true religious experiences is one of the main functions of mystical and religious traditions. Their scholars and experts are well aware of the possibility of delusory and invalid experiences, and they take pains to distinguish these from the genuine ones.[9] In a recent discussion, W. J. Wainwright has listed the following general criteria which, in Christian traditions, have been required for religious (in this case mystical) experiences to count as genuine.

(i) The consequences of the experience must be good for the mystic, in the sense of leading to or producing a new life marked by virtues such as wisdom, humility and goodness of life.

(ii) The effects of the experience must be such as tend to build up the community rather than destroy it.

(iii) The depth, profundity and the 'sweetness' (Jonathan Edwards) of what the believer says on the basis of the experience count in favour of the genuineness of that experience.

(iv) What is said on the basis of the experience ought to agree with orthodox doctrine.

(v) Resemblance of the experience to paradigm cases within the religious tradition will help establish its validity.

(vi) The judgement of spiritual authorities about the experience should be taken into account.[10]

Such tests, Wainwright suggests, are similar to those we use in ordinary cases of perception, to check that our sense-organs are

[9] See 1 John 4. 1–3; and see articles on 'Mystical Phenomena' and 'Private Revelations', in *New Catholic Encyclopaedia* (McGraw-Hill 1967). A classic Protestant discussion of the tests for valid and invalid experiences is Jonathan Edwards' *Treatise Concerning Religious Affections* (1746).

[10] William J. Wainwright, 'Mysticism and Sense Perception', in *Religious Studies*, vol. 9, no. 3. Sept. 1973, pp. 261–2.

working normally and that we are not dreaming, or suffering from an illusion.

How solid and well-founded is our knowledge of the real world anyway, we might ask? Our senses can and do deceive us. We dream, see optical illusions, imagine things, have head-noises, and so on. If it weren't for the fact that others agree with us, and the commonly accepted tests taken for granted in our society, could we be really sure that our experiences were genuine perceptions of a real world, and not just private imaginings of our own?

In the case of religious experience then, it is argued, so long as there are some accepted criteria amongst like-minded people, by which to correct momentary lapses and occasional delusions, why shouldn't religious experience be granted a similar status to sense-perception, as a source of knowledge of religious realities?

We might reply that our perceptual experience has for us a much more certain 'feel' to it than the rest of our experiences have (moral, aesthetic, or religious ones, for instance). But perhaps in thinking like that we are simply reflecting the material-istic, this-worldly prejudices of our present day society. As H. P. Owen observes, 'To a medieval Christian the existence of God was as self-evident, and belief in him as normal, as the exist-ence of, and belief in, material things.'[11] So perhaps a strong enough parallel exists between sense experience and religious experience to establish at least a *prima facie* case for the latter resembling the former in being cognitive (i.e. capable of grasping knowledge of a real object).

The argument has been made as strong as possible by empha-sizing the similarities between sensory experience of the world and religious experience (supposedly) of God. But there are important differences to be considered as well. The following four questions will serve to bring out the differences and show the weaknesses of the sense-perception model, as a basis for a convincing argument from religious experiences.

WHERE DO THE AGREED CRITERIA FOR VALID RELIGIOUS
EXPERIENCES COME FROM?

It has been suggested that reasonably clear criteria exist in both cases, for distinguishing valid from invalid, veridical from delu-

[11] *The Christian Knowledge of God* (Athlone Press 1969), p. 271.

sory experiences. In the case of sense experience these are matters of common knowledge. Everyone learns, in one way or another, that rainbows can't be touched, that reflections don't really exist behind the mirror, that departing trains do not actually shrink in size, and so on. Though no two people would put this common knowledge into words in exactly the same way, it lies behind all our everyday experiences and is hardly open to dispute.

In the case of religious experiences the situation is very different. Religious people may like to think that the commonly agreed criteria belonging to their particular tradition represent a reliable guide to religious realities. But others in different traditions, or with no particular respect for the judgement of theological and ecclesiastical experts of the past, could well ask why those, and not some quite different criteria, ought to be regarded as reliable ones.

After all, lists of 'criteria' could be drawn up according to all kinds of principles, and experiences might be found to fit them. Common agreement within a community of interest *may* show them to be sharing similar experiences of a real and persisting state of affairs. But on the other hand, agreement in interpreting might simply be the result of ignorance of alternatives, the silencing of dissidents, shared erroneous beliefs, or the similar effects of similar techniques used in producing the relevant experiences. It is clearly not enough simply to appeal to unanimous opinions within a like-minded group or tradition, as showing that their experiences are genuinely based in reality.

Broad notes that where more or less similar experiences are shared by a wide range of people, in different times and circumstances, the fact of common agreement *may or may not* count in favour of the experiences being cognitive ones.

Now, when we find that there are certain experiences which, though never very frequent in a high degree of intensity, have happened in a high degree among a few men at all times and places; and when we find that, in spite of differences in detail which we can explain, they involve certain fundamental conditions which are common and peculiar to them; two alternatives are open to us; (i) we may suppose that these men are in contact with an aspect of reality which is not revealed to ordinary persons in their everyday experience. And we may suppose that the characteristics which they agree in ascribing

45

to reality on the basis of these experiences probably do belong to it. Or (ii) we may suppose that they are all subject to a delusion from which other men are free.[12]

Likemindedness, in other words, may be a sign of genuine cognition. But on the other hand it may simply indicate a shared mistake. And the more divergent groups of people there are, the less 'agreement' within a group seems to prove anything.

WHAT KINDS OF AGREEMENT COUNT?

Broad next offers three examples of cases in which experiences shared by a like-minded group, but not universally available, have to be evaluated as veridical or delusory. The *first* example is that of trained microscopists, who are able to distinguish minute changes in the structure of cells which could not be perceived by people without a long training in the use of the microscope. We have little hesitation in taking the word of such people for the realities of the microscopic world they explore, even though it is for the present a closed one to us. The *second* example relates to 'persons of all races who habitually drink alcohol to excess'. There may well be striking similarities in the things they seem to see when heavily intoxicated (snakes, pink rats, and spiders are the usual examples, at least in the philosophical folklore on the subject). Yet we merely regard these as a uniform hallucination. The *third* example is one Broad himself constructs:

> Let us now imagine a race of beings who can walk about and touch things but cannot see. Suppose that eventually a few of them developed the power of sight. All that they might tell their still blind friends about colour would be wholly unintelligible to and unverifiable by the latter. But they would also be able to tell their blind friends a great deal about what the latter would feel if they were to walk in certain directions. These statements would be verified. This would not, of course, *prove* to the blind ones that the unintelligible statements about colour correspond to certain aspects of the world which they cannot perceive. But it would show that the seeing persons had a source of additional information about matters which the blind ones could understand and test for themselves. It

[12] Broad, *op. cit.*, p. 194.

would not be unreasonable then for the blind ones to believe that probably the seeing ones are also able to perceive other aspects of reality which they are describing correctly when they make their unintelligible statements containing colour-names.[13]

How can those three different examples help us decide how to approach the question of what kinds of agreement over religious experiences really count in assessing validity? We must first decide why we dismiss the drunkards' experiences as delusory, and whether the same reasons apply to the claims of religious mystics. The main reason is that the drunkards' supposed experience of snakes, rats, and spiders are claims which, if true, we too would readily recognize. We know exactly what to look for, what traces to expect, what sounds to listen for, and so on. Making these familiar checks and finding no supporting experiences (and knowing something too about the mind-clouding effects of alcohol), we reasonably conclude that the apparent agreement amongst drunkards is a delusion, and not the revelation of another world.

Mystics, on the other hand, tend to make claims which if true would not seriously affect the details of the material world experienced by the rest of us. So we are not so able to check and find their claims unsupported, as we are with the drunkards. We cannot, then, class the mystics as deluded according to the usual tests. On the other hand, we have not yet good reasons for accepting their claims without question.

What about the trained microscopists? What is there about them that makes us so willing to credit them with veridical experiences, even though we cannot ourselves have those experiences? Broad suggests two reasons. First, we are in a position, from simple observations we can all make, to learn sufficient about the workings of lenses and their function in microscopes to know that it would be possible for trained operators to make real discoveries, and not merely share common delusions. Second, we have mostly had sufficient experience of increasing our own perceptual skills through training and learning new techniques for it to be reasonable for us to admit the effectiveness of the training microscopists receive and the techniques they use.

Turning again to religious experience, Broad continues:

[13] *Ibid.*, pp. 194–5.

47

Now religious experience is not in nearly such a strong position as this. We do not know much about the laws which govern its occurrence and determine its variations. No doubt there are certain standard methods of training and meditation which tend to produce mystical experiences. These have been elaborated to some extent by certain Western mystics and to a very much greater extent by Eastern yogis. But I do not think that we can see here, as we can in the case of the microscopes and the training which is required to make the best use of them, any conclusive reason why these methods should produce veridical rather than delusive experiences. Uniform methods of training and meditation would be likely to produce more or less similar experiences, whether these experiences were largely veridical or wholly delusive.[14]

Broad goes on to consider his analogy of the blind men, some of whom gained the power of sight, arguing that it fits the case of those who have religious experiences reasonably well; at least well enough to give some basis for thinking their experiences to be veridical unless there are positive reasons for thinking they are not. We shall consider his conclusion later, but first closer attention must be paid to his analogy.

HOW GOOD IS THE BLIND/SIGHTED ANALOGY?

Broad suggests the analogy not to demonstrate that religious experience is a kind of extra sense that some have and others lack, but to say that if it were, that could explain how it is that vast numbers even of intelligent and informed people disagree radically over the importance they attach to religious experiences. Is it because some perceive what others simply cannot perceive?

As the blind/sighted analogy is an attractive one for believers (since they often do feel that they perceive dimensions of truth that non-believers are blind to) it is important that it be thought through carefully, so as not to confuse the main question at issue. For that question, after all, is the vital philosophical one raised by religious experience. Is what seems to be perception of a supernatural reality actually anything more than a deeper appreciation of the ordinary world, experienced with the help of certain religious images and stories?

[14] *Ibid.*, p. 196.

The believer argues that non-believers do not know God because they fail to experience his reality for themselves. They are like the blind, who do not know colour (it is assumed) because they are unable to experience it at first hand. The fact that a blind person cannot experience colour, it is argued, does not count against our knowledge that colours exist. That is the key point in the analogy—for by parallel reasoning it is claimed that the existence of non-believers does not count against the believer's knowledge that God exists.

In the case of colour, however, it is not correct to assume that the blind, simply because they lack the experience, know nothing at all on the subject. For what is it to know colour? It includes knowing that a green banana is unripe, black toast is burnt, grey skies are dreary, purple shoes are dressy. It is to be aware that bright clothes are worn at parties, sober ones at funerals; that strawberries and tomatoes are rather alike (though not in shape, size or texture), that you can paint over pink with one coat of brown (but not vice versa), and that there are dozens of different ways of being green (though they are all alike). A blind person can be aware of all that, and of the countless other ways things are sorted, matched, chosen, and changed by colours. He has all that knowledge about colour because he can understand and actively share in the talk and behaviour of everyday life, even without having colour-experiences himself.

The point of all this for the blind/sighted analogy, used in relation to religious experience, is this. The believer is taking a great deal for granted, if he thinks he knows something the unbeliever does not know, simply because he has experiences the unbeliever does not seem to have. Whereas in the case of knowing colour there is a good deal of agreed knowledge about the differences colours make which both blind and sighted can share, that does not seem to be the case with the differences religious experiences are supposed to make. For even amongst those who *have* religious experiences there are all kinds of disagreements as to what is to be learnt from those experiences.

The believer has claimed that the fact of non-believers in the world does not upset his confidence in his beliefs, since their lack of religious experiences no more counts against the reality of God than the existence of blind people counts against the reality of colours. But to know that God is real in the way we know that colours are real (a way unaffected by the existence of blind people) is not just a matter of a sufficiently large number of people having experiences taken to be of God. It requires also that those experiences are related in systematic ways, are able to be reflected in language, and are so connected to our other experiences that they form a body of knowledge which even those *without* the experiences can be capable of learning about and appreciating to some extent (as the blind can learn about and to some extent appreciate colour).

It turns out, then, that the blind/sighted analogy, to be effective for the believer in explaining away the fact that others do not have his experiences, requires of him a great deal more than just the having of (supposed) experiences of God. It requires him already to know a good deal about God, even apart from the experiences—the differences God's reality makes, the ways of connecting experiences of God to other experiences, the relevance of talk about God to the rest of life, and so on. Otherwise the believer is in nothing like the same position, *vis à vis* the non-believer, as the sighted person is *vis à vis* the blind.

Broad takes account of the need for something more than just the having of experiences, by referring to the sighted 'being able to tell their blind friends a great deal about what the latter would feel if they were able to walk in certain directions'. The sighted, in other words, may be able to make predictions which the blind can follow and discover to be true. This makes it much more reasonable for them to accept that the sighted *are* aware of things they themselves do not experience.

In the religious parallel to the blind/sighted situation, Broad suggests that the believers may be able to make predictions of an idealistic and moral kind. If non-believers take these seriously and find them to be reliable, they then may have reason to think more highly of the experiences the believers have had, which they themselves lack.

It might be said that many ideals of conduct and ways of life, which we can all recognize now to be good and useful, have been introduced into human history by the founders of religions. These persons have made actual ethical discoveries which others can afterwards recognize to be true. It might be said that this is at least roughly analogous to the case of the seeing men telling the still blind men of facts which the latter could and did verify for themselves. And it might be said that this makes it reasonable for us to attach some weight to what founders of religions tell us about things which we cannot understand or verify for ourselves; just as it would have been reasonable for the blind men to attach some weight to the unintelligible statements which the seeing men made to them about colours.[15]

The blind/sighted analogy, when carefully presented, clearly has its attractions for the defender of religion. Broad concludes, 'I think that this argument deserves a certain amount of respect, though I should find it hard to estimate how much weight to attach to it.'[16] As with many analogies used in arguments, however, we seem to need to know whether the argument succeeds independently of the blind/sighted analogy, before we can be at all sure whether the analogy is really a sound one, or whether it is misleading and inadequate.

WHY IS SENSE-PERCEPTION SO DIFFERENT?

For all the similarities that can be suggested between our sense-experiences and religious experiences, there is a simple difference, not usually seriously enough considered when the comparison is drawn. It is the fact of our having sense organs which we can study and understand in the former case, and the lack of anything at all similar in the latter. Discussions of the sense-perception analogy too often proceed as though all we have to deal with are our sense-experiences, the conclusions we reach about the real world, and the degree to which other people agree with those conclusions. If our actual sense organs are mentioned at all, they are likely to be treated simply as incidental to the business of checking and testing our experiences by agreed criteria.

It should be obvious however that the available tests and criteria are possible only because of what our sense organs are like, their location in time and space, the discriminations they enable us to make, and their complex interrelationships. The fact that we have several sense organs is itself vitally important. While we can make mistakes and misread the evidence of our senses (as we sometimes put it), we usually discover for ourselves that we have done so by one or more of our other senses.

[15] *Ibid.*, pp. 196–7.
[16] *Ibid.*, p. 197; for further criticisms of the blind/sighted analogy, see C. B. Martin, *Religious Belief* (Cornell 1959).

It looks like sugar; taste it and see. Is it smoke or steam—smell and find out. It may look safe enough, but don't touch it, it could be hot! The sense-perception model of experience, which we have so far discussed, is dominated by the experience of seeing, with not nearly enough attention paid to how much the other senses continually amend or confirm our visual experiences (which are the most prone of all to illusions). For we use several senses in exploring a doubtful situation, changing our point of view, repeating tests, and checking up on our own sensory equipment (e.g. pinching ourselves to make sure we are not dreaming). And of course we draw on the senses of other people. 'Did the clock really strike three then?' 'Was that a black swan flying past, or am I seeing things?'

Our certainty that the world is much the way we perceive it is not, then, just a product of one channel of experience supported by public agreement. It results from the combined data of five senses along with the battery of public checks and tests that go with them. Take those tests away, or reduce the number of senses allowed to function normally, and then what happens to the distinction between reality and illusion?

Sense organs are important to the situation not merely because they provide a means of testing our beliefs about the world, but because the means of testing they provide is one we can investigate and understand. We do not have to draw our criteria for reliable sense experiences simply from consensus or tradition, for we understand a good deal nowadays, and are learning more and more, about the very processes involved in the production of our sense experiences. There is simply nothing to compare with this fact in the case of religious experience, in so far as it is treated as a further form of perception parallel in some ways to sense perception.

Those forms of the perceptual analogy which try to make sense experience and religious experience seem very similar may in fact be relying too much on an obsolete view of sense perception. Modern philosophers are increasingly recognizing that giving philosophical accounts of our sense perception cannot be carried on in isolation from the psychological and physiological discoveries about the mechanisms of perception, including not only the sense organs themselves but also the causal connections between external stimuli and the brain, through the nervous system.

This is not meant to imply that sense perception must be

considered an entirely physical matter. That is a different question altogether. But there is no doubt that the physical structure and workings of our sensory equipment can give us a far greater understanding of how it is that we can make the successful tests and reliable predictions that we usually can, about the world we perceive.[17] Some of those processes (like the focusing of the eyes in stereoscopic vision) are understood, and others no doubt will be, confirming the reliability of our senses, by explaining how they operate. Sense perception, then, is very different from any other kind of perception or experience we may have.

How valid, then, is an argument from religious experiences based on the sense-perception model? The most it seems able to do is to encourage an openness to the *possibility* that those who have religious experiences may be 'on to something real'. Thus after considering various possible psychological explanations which appear to discredit religious experience (Broad argues that on the whole they do not—see below, chapter 6) he concludes,

It is reasonable to think that the concepts and beliefs of even the most perfect religions known to us are extremely inadequate to the facts which they express; that they are highly confused and are mixed up with a great deal of positive error and sheer nonsense; and that, if the human race goes on and continues to have religious experiences and reflect on them, they will be altered and improved almost out of recognition. But all this could be said, *mutatis mutandis,* of scientific concepts and theories. The claim of any particular religion or sect to have complete or final truth on these subjects seems to be too ridiculous to be worth a moment's consideration. But the opposite extreme of holding that the whole religious experience of mankind is a gigantic system of pure delusion seems to me to be almost (though not quite) as far-fetched.[18]

Such a conclusion no doubt gives some consolation to the believer, and will perhaps make the sceptic think again; but it is a long way from what most people who argue from religious experience would hope themselves to be demonstrating.

[17] See article on 'Perception' by R. J. Hirst, in *Encyclopaedia of Philosophy,* ed. Paul Edwards (Collier-Macmillan 1967), vol. 6, pp. 79ff.
[18] Broad, *op. cit.*, pp. 200–1.

The sense-perception model gives the impression that if God is to be known, it will be through experiences of a private and psychological kind, additional to physical sensations but in some way analogous to them. Yet that seems inappropriate both to the nature of God (who, as conceived in the great religions, is usually capable of making himself known through many kinds of human experience) and also to the diversity of experiences open to being interpreted as religious. As we saw in chapter 1, religious experience includes far more than merely inner sensations and passive states of consciousness.

The comparison with sense perception, if it has any weight, seems to work best when mystical experiences are being considered. (It is these Broad has mostly in mind.) But it hardly commends itself at all when applied to such charismatic or regenerative experiences as dreams, conversions, prophetic experiences, providential events, answered prayers, or the voice of conscience. The way one 'perceives' these as religious experiences is so different from our sense perceptions that no comparison can usefully be drawn, and a quite different approach is required.

On the sense-perception model, what may be known through religious experience tends to be thought of as some sort of object or environment (like the world experienced by the senses). And the question of the validity of religious beliefs based on interpretation of experiences comes to be expressed as 'veridical or delusory?'—as if it were being asked of a sense experience or supposed perception.

But if God *is* to be perceived, in and through religious experiences, it will be only in a highly unusual sense of 'perceive'. For God is not an object or environment, in most religious thought. So an analogy with sense perception may be quite unsuited to the vast number of experiences which religious believers commonly appeal to, in arguing for the truth of their beliefs.

4

KNOWING BY EXPERIENCE

'Why all this talk about arguing from religious experience?' someone may be asking. 'If you really experience God you don't have to argue, you *know* he's real, and that's all there is to it.' As the evangelical chorus has it:

> He lives, he lives,
> Christ Jesus lives today;
> He walks with me and talks with me
> Along life's narrow way.
> He lives, he lives,
> Salvation to impart;
> You ask me how I know he lives . . .
> He lives within my heart!

Believers who sing those words do feel strongly that they *know* something that others don't, and that their knowledge comes to them through religious experience, not from reasoning and argument. It is heart knowledge, not head knowledge, they tell us. So if we are trying to do justice to the varieties of religious experience, we must take very seriously this particular type, the sense of knowledge arising from inner conviction.

It is a risky business, of course, to claim to know something and to act as though one knows for sure, if one can't give much in the way of reasons for one's claim. People have claimed to 'just *know*' (as they put it) all sorts of things. Even the most irrational and misguided things have been said and done at times with apparent certainty and complete conviction by tyrants and madmen, and by ordinary people confused by ignorance or blinded by prejudice. To have no doubts at all about one's beliefs may sometimes be more a symptom of insanity or arrogant irresponsibility than of sound thinking. Yet the believer, aware of all these risks, may still feel he has a right to say he knows because he experiences God's reality for himself.

We laugh about the person who says, 'I know I'm right; don't confuse me with arguments'. And yet there are times when we find ourselves wanting to say that too. For there *are* situations in which we feel sure that we know something, even though if asked to give a good argument to back up our claim we are at a loss to know quite how to do so. 'I *know* you're the person I spoke to on the bus yesterday.' 'I *know* I have two hands.' 'I *know* it is wrong to let that child starve.' 'I *know* that six minus four leaves two.' Our experience of being-confident-that-we-are-right in cases like those is often called *intuition*. Intuitive knowing seems to be a direct, convincing way of knowing, which needs no further argument. And it is a perfectly ordinary, everyday occurrence as those examples show.

Are there such things as intuitions in religious matters too? Does a similar feeling of conviction in cases of religious experience also give us the right to say we *know,* even without having to produce any further reasons or offer any additional arguments?

KNOWLEDGE FROM INTUITION

A number of British theologians and philosophers of religion have maintained, in more or less similar ways, that religious experience is a source of religious knowledge, and that the way such knowledge arises is not from reasoning or argument, but from *intuition.* God (the primary object of religious knowledge for these thinkers) is known through finite things—events and experiences in time and space. (Human beings could not otherwise have any contact with God.) But he is known directly, in and through such media. His reality is not arrived at merely as the conclusion of an argument based upon them.

The writers who present this position begin by drawing attention to the important part played by direct, intuitive awareness in other areas of our knowledge, areas that are well established and beyond dispute. They then argue that an intuitive awareness arising through religious interpretations of experience can also be claimed as a way of knowing, though in this case it is knowledge of God that the intuition grasps.

The argument has been very thoroughly presented recently by H. P. Owen in *The Christian Knowledge of God.*[1] Owen argues

[1] Athlone Press 1969. See also H. D. Lewis, *Our Experience of God* (Allen and Unwin 1959), Fontana edn 1970, and Illtyd Trethowan, *Mysticism and Theology* (Geoffrey Chapman 1975).

56

that intuition is necessary for our grasp of the material world through the experiences our sense organs give us. It is present also when we experience other people not just as visible, tangible, moving bodies, but as conscious selves with minds and feelings like our own. There are several similarities, Owen suggests, between our intuitive awareness of other people and the believer's intuitive knowledge of God. They can be summed up thus:

(a) Just as a human person reveals his inner nature through his outer acts, so God reveals himself to us in the created order.

(b) Just as there are special moments in which another person's inner self stands out and challenges our attention, so God is known most clearly by his special revelation in Christ.

(c) Just as a human person's acts reveal both his existence as a self and something of his character, so through God's signs in nature and within our experience we learn both of his existence and, to some extent, of his character.

(d) Just as we intuitively grasp that another person is a subject and agent who brings about both physical and spiritual (or mental) effects, so we apprehend God who creates both material and spiritual realities.

In all these respects, our intuition of the reality of God, like our intuition of other selves, has a 'mediated immediacy'. It is not the product of reasoning or inference, but is none the less mediated by finite things and experiences: in the one case bodily movements, words, behaviour—in the other, general features of the natural world suggesting a divine creator, and particular religiously significant experiences.

Of course the intellectual activity of the mind, as well as the intuitive, has its part to play. It may clear the way for the intuition and provide suitable concepts (names, descriptions, interpretations, etc.) so as to make it expressible and able to be related to a wider body of knowledge. But first and foremost, none the less, it is by intuition through religious experience that God is known.

The basic form of Christian experience is the apprehension of God to which I have given the names of 'intuition' and

57

'faith'. All forms of experience are modes of this one fundamental form; they are all expressions of this primary awareness.[2]

Having taken care of the basic issue of knowledge by appealing to an intuition of the reality of God, Owen treats all cases
of genuine religious experiences as forms of that knowledge.
(In a similar way, once we have accepted that there *are* other
people, the sense of their reality persists in all our experiencing
of their bodily actions without argument or reasoning being
needed to justify it.)

The sense of God's reality, in Owen's view, underlies all other
Christian experience, i.e. experience under Christian interpretations. The basic intuition of God may arise in many ways.

> The sense of God's reality can occur in various contexts. It
> can be produced by the contemplation of beauty and order
> in nature, by meditation on the words of Scripture, by parti-
> cipation in the Church's liturgy, by some event within our
> personal existence. Yet it may not have any assignable cause
> or channel; it may come uninvited. And although it is more
> likely to occur in moods of quiet recollection, it can also
> occur when our minds are troubled by the secular pressures
> of life.[3]

The idea of knowing God by intuition through religious
experience is an attractive one for Christians, and it seems quite
consistent with the teachings of the Bible about how God is
known. Throughout the Bible God is viewed as personal, as
one who communicates, draws near, and seeks fellowship with
mankind, making himself known through natural things and in
the lives and experiences of people. The world is the medium
of his revealing activity, and by his gracious activity (the
initiative he takes in approaching humanity for its own good)
natural things and experiences become signs and symbols
through which he is known. As one theologian puts it:

> Because nature is God's and He is its creator, it lends itself
> to His use, and He can make its natural elements to speak

[2] Owen, *op. cit.,* p. 191.
[3] Owen, *op. cit.,* pp. 192–3.

sacramentally to us; not in the sense of a 'natural theology' which can *prove* the purpose of God from a mere contemplation of nature, but in the sense that God by His Word can use, and therefore we by our faith can use, natural objects . . . as sacramental expressions of His mercy and faithfulness.[4]

Not only does the knowledge-of-God-by-intuition approach fit well with biblical views of the ways God reveals himself, it also enables an account to be given of the human response to God, which is usually called *faith*. Faith, on this view, becomes a way of knowing as an intuitive response. It is not a kind of stretched belief, or assent to a set of dogmas without sufficient evidence. It is the basic intuitive awareness of God experienced as actively approaching mankind and seeking the human response of acknowledgement and trust. Another noted Christian theologian sets out the relation between revelation and faith in this way:

> The essential content of revelation is . . . God Himself, and not general truths about God or the universe or immortality or the way of duty; though such truths are implicit in the divine self-giving, as this is mediated ever more richly to the responsive soul in the changing situations of life, and are capable of reflective formulation.
> And the proper response to revelation is . . . faith, faith being not an intellectual assent to general truths, but the decisive commitment of the whole person in active obedience to, and quiet trust in, the divine will apprehended as rightfully sovereign and utterly trustworthy at one and the same time.[5]

The knowledge a believer has of God, on this view, is a living awareness of a direct, intuitive kind. It may arise in different situations and be kept alive by many different kinds of experience, but for the person who has it, it requires no further argument or support.

[4] D. M. Baillie, *The Theology of the Sacraments* (Faber 1964 edn), pp. 45–6.
[5] H. H. Farmer, *The World and God* (Nisbet 1935), Fontana edn 1963, p. 85.

Despite its careful presentation by writers such as Farmer, Lewis, and Owen and its wide appeal in popular Christian thinking, the position considered in the previous section has seemed particularly unconvincing to some recent philosophical critics.[6] This is not to be put down simply to their scepticism about things religious. Rather, it relates to the fatal weakness, in their eyes, of reliance on *intuition* as a way of knowledge that can be appealed to in the case of God or the objects of religious belief.

The criticism of this position often begins with the making of a distinction between two kinds of certainty, which are sometimes called *psychological* certainty and *rational* certainty. Certainty is a much-disputed notion in philosophy. But we can get at the main point, for our purposes, simply by comparing the difference between 'feeling certain' and 'being right'.

It is obvious, after a moment's thought, that one can feel certain without being right. I may, for instance, feel certain that it is half past three, after looking at my watch (which is usually right). But I won't go on feeling certain if I discover that for once the watch has stopped. In other words, I can check the appropriateness of my feeling of certainty against the rightness of the watch. But I can't check the rightness of the watch against my feeling of certainty. The feel of certainty is not what makes us right, even though we may often have a feel of certainty when we *are* right.

Being right then is not a matter of having some recognizable state of mind, a sense or feeling of certainty. It is a matter of our beliefs and states of mind standing in some appropriate relation to various states of affairs.

Many of the problems associated with 'feeling certain' go also with the idea of having intuitive knowledge. The sense of 'having an intuition that such-and-such is the case' may possess a quality of clarity or conviction or a peculiar directness in some circumstances. I may feel very strongly, for instance, that I am being watched, or that something disastrous or momentous

[6] In particular, see R. W. Hepburn, *Christianity and Paradox* (Watts 1958); C. B. Martin, 'A Religious Way of Knowing', in *New Essays in Philosophical Theology*, ed. Antony Flew and Alasdair MacIntyre (SCM Press 1955); Antony Flew, *God and Philosophy* (Hutchinson 1966), ch. 6.

is about to happen. Perhaps these feelings turn out to be justified at times. What we felt certain about, intuitively, was actually so. Such cases, taken along with the everyday cases of intuitive knowing mentioned above, may tempt us to conclude that *having an intuition* has a recognizable feel about it, that can be taken as a reliable sign of being right, whatever the circumstances.

But then the following question arises. If you have *only* the intuitive feeling of certainty to go on, how do you know in a given case that you are having *that* feeling (i.e. the one that counts as a sign of intuitions)? Perhaps your memory of 'the intuitive feel' is letting you down this time. It is not enough to say you feel certain that your memory is right; for that is just repeating the process—using an intuition to check intuition itself. And if *whatever* seems right can be right, what does 'getting it right (or wrong)' mean?

The reliability of our 'sense of intuition' is not something to be taken for granted, then, as an independent guide to genuine knowledge. There's no doubt that we have reliable intuitions in some situations. But it is the situation, not the feeling of intuition, that determines whether or not intuition is a reliable way of knowing in these cases. Even in the case of our intuitive knowledge of other people (on which the argument for religious intuition so heavily relies) the feeling that we have profound and certain knowledge may be quite false. As Bertrand Russell wrote,

> One of the most notable examples of intuition is the knowledge people believe themselves to possess of those with whom they are in love. The wall between different personalities seems to become transparent, and people think they see into another soul as into their own. Yet deception in such cases is constantly practised with success; and even where there is no intentional deception, experience gradually proves, as a rule, that the supposed insight was illusory, and that the slower more groping methods of the intellect are in the long run more reliable.[7]

Those are some of the difficulties which face anyone who argues from what seems to be an intuitive awareness, in religious experience, to the conclusion that there really is knowledge of God. It is not enough to emphasize the sense of certainty or

[7] *Mysticism and Logic* (Longmans Green & Co. 1919), p. 16.

directness of the basic religious experience by giving it descriptions like 'awareness', 'encounter', 'apprehension', or 'response'. For those terms take it for granted that there *is* a genuine object of experience, beyond the experiencer's own mental states. But that is the very question at issue.

Nor does it seem sufficient to point out, as Owen does, that we accept intuitive, non-inferential knowledge in such everyday areas as sense perception, or awareness of other minds. For as we saw (chapter 3) the case of sense perception is a special one. Our knowledge of the workings of sense organs, and the range of tests and checking procedures which surround the experiences they give us, all contribute to the context in which our intuitive perceptions take place and help us to justify them. Similarly with our awareness of other people as being conscious, and not as mere moving bodies. For we have, after all, a body ourselves. And while our awareness of others may at times be largely intuitive it is capable of being backed up with a strong argument from analogy, from our knowledge of ourselves as conscious beings.

But when we turn to some other areas in which people rely on intuitions (morality, child-rearing, archaeological exploration, or fortune-telling, for instance) it is much more difficult to say whether the sense of having such-and-such an intuition is a sure sign of knowing or being right. The nature of those subjects is such that rules for making sound judgements and ways of avoiding self-deception are far less well established. How can appealing to intuition make up for those deficiencies? And is religion any better off, with all its variety and openness to disagreement? The idea of knowing purely by intuition seems to become less and less plausible the more the fact of religious diversity is faced. Aren't there just too many different intuitions being had, by too many people, for intuition on its own to be a reliable guide to the truth?

Just because we have *some* acceptable cases of knowing by intuition (sense perception, other minds, simple arithmetic) it does not follow that there is an intuitive 'way of knowing' open to be used in other cases as well. To assume that is like assuming that because someone is able to read road-signs and to read newspapers, they will also be able to read palms. But what counts as being able to read palms is not an agreed-upon matter, in the way the reading of road-signs and newspapers is; and therefore it is quite unclear whether the other kinds of reading abilities have anything in common with palm-reading at all. Similarly, what counts as having knowledge of God is so much in doubt and dispute that until agreement is reached on that question, there is no sound basis for deciding whether such knowledge could or could not be arrived at through intuitions, even if intuitions *are* reliable in certain other cases of knowledge.

Of course Owen, Lewis, and the other thinkers who appeal to intuitive knowledge of God have not intended to produce a short-cut argument for the truth of Christianity based on the view that the believer simply *knows* and that's all there is to it. There is far more in their position than that. They offer very comprehensive accounts of the interplay of experiences, interpretations, doctrines, traditions, imagination, and action which make up religious life as a whole. Their aim is to describe and analyse the total Christian enterprise in such a way that it commends itself as an interpretation of the world and the experiences of human life.

But the central place given to a basic, not-argued-for intuition of God in their overall position does invite serious criticisms from philosophers for whom intuition seems a very weak straw to be clutching at.

Yet for all the possible criticisms, it doesn't follow at all that what people think are experiences of God must all be illusory. Nor has it been shown that the person who says 'I know he lives—he lives within my heart' is talking simple-minded nonsense. *If* a religion like Christianity is true, it is very likely that there are situations in which people are directly aware of God's reality and activity, within the experiences and situations of life. But it is the *if*, in the previous sentence, that highlights the difficulty, for the philosopher at least. While *that* question is still open, how can he decide whether people's impressions that they are intuitively aware of God should be regarded as reliable?

KNOWLEDGE ABOUT AND EXPERIENCE OF

Theologians who argue that God is known by immediate encounter rather than by inference and argument rest their claim on a view of the special features of person-to-person knowledge. Meeting someone at first hand, they remind us, is very different from merely knowing about them. And encountering someone as another conscious person seems to involve a rather special kind of knowledge quite different from our knowledge of them as an object or thing.

The religious philosopher Martin Buber in his book *I and Thou* has given a widely influential account of that difference. He begins:

> The world is twofold for man in accordance with his twofold attitude.
> The attitude of man is twofold in accordance with the two basic words he can speak
> The basic words are not single words but word pairs.
> One basic word is the pair I-You
> The other basic word is the pair I-It.[8]

I-You relationships are direct, reciprocal, person-to-person. They contain no reasoning or reflection and though deeply profound are fragile and impermanent. The world of It—of objectivity, reasoning, analysis—is unavoidable and human beings cannot live without it. But whoever lives only in the world of It, Buber tells us, does not become truly human.

Buber and other personalistic thinkers have encouraged theologians to point also to the biblical tradition in which, as we have seen, God is personal and seeks person-to-person relations with human beings whom he has created. If God is conceived of as personal, then we must think in I-You rather than I-It terms in seeking to experience God, they say. So great stress is placed in theology on the difference between thinking or arguing about God on the one hand, and experiencing God in personal existential encounter on the other.

That contrast is easily related to other familiar contrasts in Christian thought. For instance, belief *in* is taken to be better than belief *about*. Faith is recommended, rather than speculation, in approaching God. Involvement and trust are encouraged, rather than detachment and theorizing. A wealth of religiously suggestive parallels can be drawn, all resting on the basic distinction between knowledge *about* God (an I-It matter) and experience *of* God (an I-You experience).

A further feature of I-You, rather than I-It, relationships is the impression that much of what we know in a personal encounter can't be put into words. Thus C. E. Raven writes,

[8] *I and Thou*, a new tr. by Walter Kaufmann (Scribners 1970), p. 53.

64

As soon as we treat a human being not as a thing but as a person we discover in him elements that we can apprehend but not describe. It is only on the surface that we can define one another; even when, as we say, we know our friends through and through, share their impulses and react to their every mood, yet such knowledge when we try to express it remains ultimately mysterious: 'I know but cannot tell'.[9]

This inexpressibility at the heart of an interpersonal relationship further supports the view that if God is to be known, relationships with him will inevitably have features appropriate to an I-You rather than an I-It encounter. Why should we expect genuine knowledge of God to be any more capable of analysis, description, or reasoned argument than genuine person-to-person knowledge is? Questions of reasoning or analysis have no application to the profound experiences of meeting and encounter, we are told. Indeed, if one attempts in a moment of encounter to describe or analyse the person encountered, the I-You relation is immediately broken and the other party experienced only as an It.

Because the idea of encountering God in religious experience is so familiar a notion to Christian believers and so consistent with the biblical ways of speaking, anyone relying on this way of speaking needs to be very much aware of the philosophical problems it raises. For as in the case of the supposed intuitive knowledge of God, this closely-related idea of knowledge through encounter has been subjected to some telling criticisms. Arising from the criticisms, three points need to be discussed.

(i)   The sense that an encounter is taking place may be mistaken.
(ii) Having 'experience of' presupposes having knowledge about.
(iii) 'Experience of' is not in itself knowledge.

(i)   THE 'SENSE OF ENCOUNTER' MAY BE MISTAKEN

This is similar to the problem about intuition and the feeling of certainty. It is not that our sense of such things is *never* reliable. But the surrounding of possible checks and tests that show it to be reliable in one context may simply not be there in another context, and then the mere impression of certainty is no guide at all for us to go by.

[9] *Natural Religion and Christian Theology* (Cambridge 1953), p. 47.

As Bertrand Russell reminded us, our apparent intuitions about other people can be wildly astray. The same is true of the sense of a 'genuine I-You encounter'. We all have experiences of shared awareness with close friends, in which 'knowledge about' fades into the background, and person-to-person communion or *rapport* is achieved. At such times neither person seems to be treated as an It. Each may think he has genuinely become a You in the eyes of the other. Yet how do we know when such an encounter has really been achieved? Is the impression that it is taking place enough to go on?

Standard situations in plays or on television remind us how easily what seems to be a genuine I-You relationship can turn out to be something quite different. A chattering wife talks to her husband who has fallen asleep or has put the telephone receiver on the desk while he continues his work. A spy reveals secrets to a trusted friend who is an unsuspected double agent. In classic cases of disguise such as those in *Twelfth Night* or *The Marriage of Figaro,* everybody but the victim of the deception knows what the real facts are. Misinterpreted encounters, then, far from being impossible, are not at all rare.

Up to this point the critic's position may not amount to much more than the caution, 'You may not be as right as you think you are', in treating what seems to be an encounter as a genuine experience of God. The fact that some supposed encounter with God could possibly be mistaken won't much worry a believer if he is convinced that he is right in fact. There is more to the sceptic's position, however, as appears in the next point we must consider.

(ii) HAVING 'EXPERIENCE OF' PRESUPPOSES HAVING 'KNOWLEDGE ABOUT'

Preachers and theologians often point out that 'know', in the biblical and religious sense, is a much richer notion than simply 'possess knowledge about'. It involves an I-You, not an I-It relationship. Thus when Adam 'knew his wife Eve' (Genesis 4.1) there was a good deal more to it than simply his possessing the information that such-and-such a female person existed. Religious knowing, like person-to-person knowing, is not just a possession of facts or information. It is an experience of total involvement.

Knowledge in the biblical sense of the word is not theoretical contemplation but an entering into subjective relations as between person and person—relations of trust, obedience, respect, worship, love, fear, and so on. It is knowledge in the sense of our knowledge of other persons rather than of our knowledge of objects, 'existential' rather than 'scientific' knowledge.[10]

If believers genuinely do have a direct encounter with God, then, it is quite inappropriate to try to force that experience into the mould of scientific information or knowledge about— expecting them to provide accurate descriptions or meet objective tests. Surely we know well enough from our experience of personal knowledge that such an approach is bound to be negative and fruitless.

But even granting that scientific, impersonal 'knowledge about' isn't the most important thing in interpersonal relations, we must not conclude that it is quite irrelevant and can be done without. After all, Adam's knowledge about Eve is there in the background all the time, so to speak. It may not seem very important to him when she is right beside him, and his interest is in something more I-You than mere factual information. But suppose Adam has never actually met Eve, and has only the odd trace (a slender footprint, a strand or two of hair) to go by, in deciding whether there is anyone other than himself in the world. The possibility of external, objective information will then be by far the more important question for him. For without Eve's existence as an It being established, there is no question at all of her being encountered as a You.

So 'mere factual knowledge' is by no means as unimportant to personal, existential knowledge as the contrast between I-You and I-It may suggest. In the same way, it is too easily taken for granted, in making a contrast between knowing about God and personally encountering him, that 'knowledge about' is largely unproblematic and readily available, and that its only defect is that it lacks immediacy and depth by contrast with genuine, interpersonal experience of God.

To the philosophical onlooker at least, knowledge about God is the very thing that is in question. It is largely because it might be a source of knowledge about God, that religious

[10] Alan Richardson, *An Introduction to the Theology of the New Testament* (SCM Press, 1958), p. 40.

67

experience is being investigated at all. So even though the preacher or believer may not rate 'knowledge about' as highly as 'experience of', the philosopher would be more than content if even the former could be established for certain.

That is not to say, of course, that the philosopher demands objective, scientific knowledge of God before contemplating the possibility that anyone might have a direct, interpersonal awareness of God. If a certain religious tradition holds that God is not to be thought of as an It, then it is up to the philosopher to respect that feature of the concept of God. But isn't it on this very point that encounters with God differ so much from encounters with people? For at least so far as establishing their existence goes, people *are* open to being investigated and known about as Its, however much we may prefer (at times) to be encountering them as Yous.

In the case of people we certainly can have I-It relationships without I-You ones. But could we have an I-You encounter that did not seriously depend on a background of I-It knowledge? (Who would we take the 'You' we were experiencing to be, if we knew nothing about him?) Similarly in the case of a religious experience believed to be an I-You encounter with God, unless the believer was in a position to supplement the experience with a good deal of already available knowledge about God (that he is creator of the world, for instance, judge of all men, father of Jesus Christ, etc.) his belief 'I am personally encountering God' would mean no more than 'I am experiencing a profound personal encounter with someone I know not who'. Without knowledge about what is being experienced, experience *of* points no more towards God than towards any other possible person.[11]

(iii) 'EXPERIENCE OF' IS NOT IN ITSELF KNOWLEDGE

Suppose it were indisputable that God is genuinely experienced in some form of first-hand awareness. It does not follow that such first-hand experience or encounter, *on its own*, would count as knowledge at all. The point can be put this way. We generally think that someone who has experienced something for

[11] Difficulties in 'encounter theology' are explored in greater detail by R. W. Hepburn in *Christianity and Paradox* chs. 3 and 4; and see Frederick Ferré, *Language, Logic and God* (Eyre & Spottiswoode 1962), ch. 8.

himself is in a better position to know the truth about it than someone who has not. Yet why should that be so? What does first-hand experience add, that all available second-hand knowledge cannot supply?

There are obviously some cases in which a lack of first-hand experience is unimportant, so long as there is good second-hand knowledge. A male doctor, for instance, simply cannot have first-hand experience of being pregnant; yet his knowledge about pregnancy may be far greater than that of some uninformed woman patient who is experiencing pregnancy at first hand yet understands little of what is taking place. She might still feel inclined to say that her doctor doesn't *really* know what pregnancy is, whereas she does. But what does she mean?

Perhaps a clearer case would be to compare equally well trained and experienced doctors, one a man and one a woman, the latter of whom has also given birth. Surely then we should say that the woman doctor has a better knowledge of what pregnancy is than the man. Well, perhaps we should—but is it merely the *experience* of pregnancy that the man lacks? There seems to be more to it than that. For what the woman doctor gains from having been pregnant is not just an additional experience, but a whole set of impressions and memories and items of information that can only be learnt by having the experience oneself.

It is the additional knowledge *about* pregnancy that being pregnant makes available, rather than the mere experience *of* pregnancy, that makes the woman doctor better off than the man. The extra knowledge she now has, though it can only be gained by having first-hand experience, is certainly not *the same thing as* that experience. Furthermore, without all her other knowledge (which she and the male doctor have acquired through training, practice, etc.) the additional lessons learnt through actually having the experience would mean nothing much to her. If she had no prior knowledge at all about pregnancies, the experience she went through would not even be recognized as a pregnancy by her, and might merely seem to be a rather lengthy and uncomfortable bodily process, ending in the surprise arrival of a baby.

First-hand experience is important then not because it *is* knowledge but because it may put us in a position to increase our knowledge. Knowledge, in other words, is not merely a matter of experiences or kinds of awareness. It consists as well

69

in what one can do with or make of those experiences in relation to the rest of one's knowledge and experience. To treat *experience of* something as itself a kind of knowing is to confuse the means by which we may gain knowledge with the content of the knowledge itself.

At this point someone may object that too much emphasis is being placed on learning, or gaining knowledge. Surely we do not seek close personal encounters with people simply for the sake of learning from those experiences more facts about them, which we could not find out so well in other ways. Our I-You encounters are for the sake of company, enjoyment, fellowship, sharing, and love. 'Knowledge about', even if we do presuppose it, is a secondary matter. And if God exists, the same is true of religious experiences taken to be I-You encounters with him. They are sought for the sake of love, worship, fellowship, not as aids to knowledge (even if knowledge may be increased through them).

> O Lord, my heart is not lifted up,
>   my eyes are not raised too high;
> I do not occupy myself with things
>   too great and too marvellous for me.
> But I have calmed and quieted my soul,
>   like a child quieted at its mother's breast;
>   like a child that is quieted is my soul.   (Psalm 131)

The objection is a sound one. If there are encounters between God and people they may be chiefly for those non-intellectual, interpersonal reasons, and not for the sake of acquiring knowledge. It is only if a claim to *know* is based on experiences taken as encounters with God, and on them alone, that the philosophical difficulties considered above apply. And the fact is that believers often do try to argue that they have knowledge of God, purely on the strength of such experiences. The effect of the philosophical criticisms has been simply to show how inadequate that kind of argument is.

The criticisms do nothing at all to show that awareness of God is illusory. They simply suggest that even if it is genuine it cannot, by itself, solve all the problems about whether or not we have good reason for belief in God.

Awareness of God, oneness with God, the sense of his presence, the inner conviction of his reality—the situations and experiences which lead people to talk in these ways are vital for religious belief. They have kept it alive in the past and continue to make it plausible for millions of people today. What such experiences do is to generate *a sense of knowing God*.

The philosophical difficulties of intuitions, encounters, mystical experiences, and other sources of that sense do not detract from its importance for religion. Religious people may conclude, 'If philosophy isn't very impressed with the sense of God, then so much the worse for philosophers. They have obviously hardened their hearts and refused to be open to God.'

But it is a mistake to react in that way. For one thing, a fair number of modern philosophers are religious believers and regard the sense of God as a central fact in their own lives. That makes it all the more important for them to give it the most careful philosophical attention. For they will not want so important an experience to be discredited by being used in weak arguments or doubtful reasoning.

The chief point of the philosophical criticisms of 'knowing God by experience' amounts to this. Where popular religious reasoning falls down is not in taking the sense of God too seriously, but in trying to treat it as a form of knowledge, of a self-certifying kind, immediately available to those who have it. Knowledge, the philosophers point out, is just not like that— whether it is knowledge of God or of anything else. The *sense* of knowing is never on its own a sufficient sign of knowledge. (That distinction is a key to many of the philosophical difficulties in claims to know God by experience.)

But if the *sense of God* fails, in the end, to count as knowledge of God, what is to be said about it? Is it of no further philosophical interest and to be discarded, like a pricked balloon, as being simply a great illusion?

Nothing that has been said in this or previous chapters leads to that conclusion. There is no justification for taking such an all-or-nothing view of religious experience (even though at times both philosophical critics and religious thinkers are inclined to do so). A critical but constructive approach to the sense of God, and to religious experience as a whole, has yet

71

to be worked out in detail amongst today's philosophers of religion. But to conclude this chapter I shall outline the general direction such an approach appears to be taking.

A great many experiences in human life produce what has come to be interpreted as 'a sense of knowing God'.[12] The occurrence of those experiences is important to questions of knowledge and truth, not because by themselves they guarantee the rightness of the interpretations given by those who experience them, but because they are the kinds of experience *which would be explained if those interpretations were correct*.

And therefore, in an indirect but real way, the experiences add weight to the overall theoretical scheme (the theology) under which they are interpreted and experienced. The task of showing that the overall scheme itself may reasonably be regarded as a body of knowledge is a far wider one. It cannot simply be dealt with by asking of any particular interpretation, 'Is it valid or invalid?' For one's estimate of the value of any particular experience will depend on how one evaluates the total belief system in terms of which that experience is thought to be significant.

It helps, then, to keep both belief system and related experiences in view when asking about the possibility of knowledge through religious experience. This approach avoids the weaknesses of appeals to special, infallible kinds of religious perceptions, intuitions, or encounters. At the same time it allows the experiences behind such appeals to be taken seriously.

Our next chapter will consider some recent philosophers of religion whose writings suggest a broad approach to evaluating religious experience in relation to the reasonableness of the belief systems and overall world-views that are based upon it.

[12] This is not to suggest that there is only one basic religious experience, nor that other interpretations are not equally interesting. But experiences interpreted as the sense of a God are sufficiently widespread and persistent to be worth treating as a prime example.

5

INTERPRETATION AND RATIONAL BELIEF

Praised be my Lord God with all his creatures,
    and specially our brother the sun,
    who brings us the day and who brings us the light;
    fair is he, and shining with a very great splendour;
    O Lord, he signifies to us thee!
Praised be my Lord for our sister, the moon, and for the stars,
    which thou hast set clear and lovely in heaven.
Praised be my Lord for our brother, the wind,
    and for air and cloud, calms, and all weather,
    by which thou upholdest in life all creatures.
Praised be my Lord for our sister, the water,
    who is very serviceable unto us
    and humble, and precious, and clean.
Praised be my Lord for our brother, fire,
    through whom thou givest us light in the darkness;
    and he is bright, and pleasant,
    and very mighty, and strong.
Praised be my Lord for our mother, the earth,
    which sustains us and keeps us
    and brings forth diverse fruits and flowers
    of many colours and grass.   St Francis of Assisi,
                                    from *The Canticle of the Creatures*

St Francis seems to experience everyday things in a very religious way. Does he really *know* anything that the non-religious person looking on the world does not know? Is it all just a way of speaking? The religious interpretation he places on the natural world no doubt teaches us a lot about him, but do we learn anything else from it as well? What is it to have a world-view, an overall way of looking at things, by which one lives?

One philosopher who has been especially interested in explaining the nature of world-views or 'ways of looking at things' is John Wisdom. There are disputes about what the world is like, Wisdom suggests, which are not to be solved by discovering more facts, but by coming to a better appreciation of what the facts as a whole show. This is illustrated, he reminds us, in the interpreting of works of art, literature, and drama (did the heroine love him, or did she really hate him underneath?); in historical judgements; in legal disputes (Had the defendant 'exercised reasonable care' or had he not?); and even in everyday arguments about whether or not a certain word fits (Is it being 'fussy' to insist that the children should clean their shoes before going to school?). Such cases show us that how things really are isn't always just a matter of 'the facts', but has to do also with the possible ways of taking or viewing them.

Religious ways of speaking, similarly, may be thought of as ways of coming to see, or ways of regarding, the facts. They are more than just a matter of words, for they can succeed in bringing to our notice patterns of significance within the facts— subtleties and hints and shades of meaning that would otherwise be missed. Thus St Francis, even if he gives us no new information in talking about the world as he does, can make us see things in new ways and thus experience them differently.

WHAT THE GARDENER STORY LEAVES OUT

One of the most thought-about and argued-over works in modern philosophy of religion is a paper entitled 'Gods', in which John Wisdom talks about alternative world-views—religious and non-religious. In that paper he tells this story. Two people return to their garden after a long absence and find among the weeds a few of the old plants surprisingly vigorous. One says to the other, 'It must be that a gardener has been coming and doing something about these plants'. They ask around but find that no neighbour has ever seen anyone at work in their garden. The former however continues to be impressed by the purposefulness and apparent feeling for beauty and design in the way things are arranged. The other reminds him of the equally obvious weeds and neglect. They examine the garden most carefully, finding further signs suggesting a gardener's care, but also signs suggesting the contrary. The point is reached where no further discovery of facts about that or any other garden settles the issue between them.

74

'At this stage,' Wisdom asks, 'what is the difference between them?' He continues:

> The one says 'A gardener comes unseen and unheard. He is manifested only in his works with which we are all familiar', the other says 'There is no gardener' and with this difference in what they say about the gardener goes a difference in how they feel towards the garden, in spite of the fact that neither expects anything of it which the other does not expect.[1]

Yet Wisdom rejects the suggestion that the only difference between the two men is that 'one calls the garden by one name and feels one way towards it, while the other calls it by another name and feels another way towards it'. There is still, he thinks, a point in asking 'Which is *right*?' Yet what could that point be?

What makes the dispute still a reasonable one, Wisdom holds, is the *procedure* which the two parties follow. It is not to be thought, he says, that once all the available facts are known there is no point in continuing the argument.

> Our two gardeners even when they had reached the stage where neither expected any experimental result which the other did not, might yet have continued the dispute, each presenting and representing the features of the garden favouring his hypothesis, that is, fitting the model for describing the accepted facts; each emphasizing the pattern he wishes to emphasize.[2]

The value of the procedure, Wisdom feels, is that it keeps alive possible judgements on the facts, and the patterns, connections, and hidden meanings within them.

Religious arguments about the world involve a similar procedure, Wisdom suggests, and thus continue to have a point. As he says in a later paper:

> The old questions 'Does God exist?' 'Does the devil exist?' aren't senseless, aren't beyond the scope of reason. On the contrary they call for new awareness of what has so long

---

[1] 'Gods', reprinted in *Logic and Language*, ed. Antony Flew (Blackwell 1951), p. 193.

[2] *Ibid.*, p. 197.

been about us, in case knowing nature so well we never know her.[3]

Much discussion has followed Wisdom's writings, a good deal of it concerned to show why, for all their suggestiveness, they seem to leave out something important about religious belief.[4] How are we to go about deciding the adequacy of Wisdom's description of the meaning of religious arguments about the world? One way is to ask what the place of religious experience is, in such a view.

Consider the gardener story again. One thing is missing, which is usually present in the parallel religious situation. It is the possibility that not only do the parties interpret the facts differently but also that the different overall views they hold will cause them to have quite different experiences. And for one of them, at least, those experiences will be very relevant to the matter in dispute. For the one who believes there is a gardener, certain things about the garden may produce reactions and responses simply not available to the other. No doubt if he tries to tell of 'a vivid awareness of the gardener himself', or 'a sense of one guiding him' as he explores the garden, his friend will dismiss these as imagination and wish-fulfilment, and not as experiences to be taken seriously. Gardeners being what they are (absent ones in particular), the friend's sceptical reaction will no doubt be thoroughly reasonable. On the other hand, God, if he exists, may have any number of ways of bringing about experiences without himself being physically present. Thus while supposed experiences of the undetectable gardener will probably be illusory, because of what we know about gardeners, it does not follow that supposed experiences of God will be. That is the question at issue.[5]

For the one who has the additional experiences, then, they will seem to count as further facts, providing solid confirmation of his beliefs. Similarly, the sense of the reality of God which arises in the course of the believer's experience of the world

[3] 'The Logic of God', in *Paradox and Discovery* (Blackwell 1965), p. 22.
[4] See, for instance, Renford Bambrough, *Reason, Truth and God* (Methuen 1969), ch. 4.
[5] Wisdom appears, in the end, to value religious experiences largely in psychological terms, with the recognition that without the religious interpretations bringing them to our attention we would never come to appreciate them. See 'Gods' pp. 202ff.

(within his religious world-view and belief-system) is not simply an accompanying feeling but becomes part of the evidence itself and is open to interpretation by the very belief-system which evokes it. It would be possible to enlarge Wisdom's story still further along the lines of Broad's analogy of the blind and the sighted, with the believer, through his supposed experience of the gardener himself, becoming better than his partner at discovering new things about the garden, explaining the point of the weeds, and so on.[6]

It is only by leaving a highly typical form of religious experience out of the picture entirely, then, that Wisdom has been able to suggest that believer and non-believer are agreed as to the facts. The situation he describes, on closer inspection, becomes less and less like that characteristic of religious belief. For unlike the believer in a gardener, who might perhaps be prepared to agree that no future facts can be expected to settle the dispute his way, the believer in God lives in hope, not only of events in a future life, but of day by day support for his convictions, in the form of further events and experiences open to religious interpretations. 'The steadfast love of the Lord never ceases, his mercies never come to an end; they are new every morning' (Lamentations 3.22–3).

When such further events and experiences occur, the two parties are no longer simply differing in their interpretations of facts on which they both agree. They are divided also in their view of what possible further facts there are. The believer takes his 'experiences of God' to be genuine and highly significant data; the non-believer regards them simply as chance occurrences or illusory feelings and therefore as not to be included amongst the relevant facts at all.

To take account of the place of religious experience in supporting belief, it follows, the difference between believer and non-believer must be seen as being something more than just the holding of different world-views. For the believer (so he supposes) is experiencing things the non-believer is not, and therefore has additional facts to take account of. Thus St Francis, as we saw, not only experiences the sun as a strong and splendid brother, but in doing so finds himself praising God for it, and saying 'O Lord, he signifies to us thee!'

[6] See Basil Mitchell, *The Justification of Religious Belief* (Macmillan 1973), p. 114.

Wisdom's gardener story, in which different readings of the same facts are made, brings to mind the experience sometimes known as a *Gestalt-shift* or *change of aspect*. This experience can be recognized from a couple of examples. Consider a sketch consisting of two straight lines crossing at right angles. The lines may be seen as two corners touching at a point, or as a cross, or even as the point of a pyramid, viewed from directly above. Again, we may see a chess-board as white with black squares on it, or as black with white squares. Some well-known picture-puzzles are based on our experiencing a change of aspect. One known as the *duck-rabbit* can be seen either as a rabbit's head facing to the left, or as a duck's head facing to the right (ears become beak, and vice versa).

The 'change of aspect' experience is sometimes thought to illustrate the difference between the believer's and the non-believer's ways of viewing the world. John Hick, for instance, writing about the possibility of knowledge through religious experience, uses as examples the duck-rabbit and other cases of 'seeing-as'. The believer, Hick argues, can discover God as lying behind the world, and experience his presence in and through it. This knowledge comes through the believer's interpreting in a new way facts that are familiar to us all. (This religious way of knowledge through interpretation, he considers, is what in religion is called *faith*.)

Beginning with the experience of seeing-as (the change of aspect experience), Hick develops a more comprehensive theory, based on the idea of *experiencing-as*.

> The next step is from these two-dimensional pictures and diagrams to experiencing-as in real life—for example, seeing the tuft of grass over there in the field as a rabbit, or the shadows in the corner of the room as someone standing there. And the analogy to be explored is with two contrasting ways of experiencing the events of our lives and of human history, on the one hand as purely natural events and on the other hand as mediating the presence and activity of God.[7]

[7] 'Religious Faith as Experiencing-As', in *Talk of God*, ed. G. N. A. Vesey (Macmillan 1969), p. 23.

The believer and the non-believer are confronted by the same physical environment, and yet it has a different nature and quality for each, a different meaning and significance. For 'one does and the other does not experience life as a continual interaction with the transcendent God'.[8]

Hick anticipates a possible objection that goes like this. When we see the duck-rabbit as a duck or as a rabbit, we already know what it is like to see ducks and rabbits. That is, our seeing-as, in the duck-rabbit case, presupposes times when we actually *see* ducks or rabbits (or unambiguous drawings of them). The same is true when we see a tuft of grass in a field as a rabbit, or shadows in the corner as a person standing there. It is only because we have previously experienced what were clearly rabbits, or people (and not tufts of grass and shadows), that we can experience something unclear as such things. And therefore, the objection continues, to suggest that the believer is 'experiencing life *as* a continual interaction with a transcendent God' presupposes that he knows what it would be like to experience (without the 'as') God in that way. But that is the very question at issue; is there such knowledge of God?

To meet the objection, Hick introduces the argument that *all* experiencing is experiencing-as, even the supposedly clear, unambiguous cases. Consider, for instance, a table fork. While to us it may seem familiar and unmistakable, it simply cannot be seen to be a fork, except by someone who possesses the concept of a fork (and not, say, by a Stone Age man). All conscious experiencing involves recognition which goes beyond what is immediately sensed; it involves interpretation according to concepts we already possess. Therefore, Hick concludes, the experiencing-as which takes place under religious interpretations is no different in principle from ordinary, everyday experiencing (though of course differences in the nature of the object experienced lead to some special peculiarities in the case of religious knowledge).

A number of philosophical criticisms have been made of the view that 'all experiencing is experiencing-as'. The main point of these amounts to a concern to distinguish two senses of the phrase 'experience-as'. The first is one which applies in cases where the thing experienced remains permanently open to two or more possible readings (as in the duck-rabbit puzzle). The second is for cases where the thing in question turns out to be

[8] *Ibid*.

79

one thing rather than another, and thereafter is simply described under the concept that fits it best (for example, when the shape in the corner turns out to be simply a shadow).

The advantage of keeping 'experience-as' for the former cases is that to do so preserves a clear contrast with more usual cases of unambiguous experiencing.[9] The point can be illustrated by considering the word 'ambiguous' itself. If we accept the suggestion that *every* experience is (in a weak sense) ambiguous, then we are stretching the use of the word so much that it is no longer useful for marking off cases which are really ambiguous (in a strong sense).

Thus to reply to the question 'How can we experience anything *as* God if we aren't sure what it is to experience God?' by saying 'Well, after all, *all* experiencing is experiencing-as' is not really to meet the objection. The duck-rabbit, change of aspect experience, and the seeing-as of something ambiguous under a specific interpretation, are both abnormal kinds of experience. They are recognizable because they contrast with normal cases of seeing and experiencing. (They are 'parasitic upon' normal cases, to use philosophers' jargon.) If even normal seeing and experiencing were seeing-as and experiencing-as, there would no longer be the contrast that leads us to those special ways of speaking in the first place.[10]

The risk of playing down the contrast between experiencing-as and normal experiencing is that it makes it harder to insist on the difference which the religious believer certainly wants to preserve; that is, the difference between taking something to be the case that really isn't the case, and taking something to be the case and being right in doing so.

We need not discuss the philosophical problems in 'experiencing-as' any further. For there is another reason for questioning Hick's approach (at least as it has been so far considered). Like Wisdom, Hick has assumed that the place to begin is with the familiar things, the shared perceptions of our world, on which believer and non-believer place their different overall interpretations. It is that assumption that makes the duck-rabbit illustration seem a useful starting-point. But this approach does not

[9] Thus the philosophers Austin and Wittgenstein each kept *seeing-as* for those special cases which contrast with normal perception.
[10] For a fuller discussion of this point, see Kai Nielsen, *Contemporary Critiques of Religion* (Macmillan 1971), pp. 79ff.

lend itself at all well to taking account of those religious experiences which arise *as a result of* holding the religious world-view. Those experiences, for the believer (though not of course for the non-believer), may be highly significant and relevant facts to be included in the total data to which his overall interpretation is applied.

We have already noted how holding a certain belief or set of beliefs about what is possible may totally alter the way one experiences things. What is also altered is the range of things one is capable of learning from those experiences. The patterns, connections, discriminations which are made possible by having in mind a comprehensive interpreting scheme greatly increase the number of meanings that can be found in things, and therefore the amount of possible information that can be acquired.

The radio listener for example, who hears certain crackles on his transistor and takes them to be simply atmospheric static, may well be perceiving the same sounds as the coastguard who is listening for signals from a missing yacht. But when the latter detects within the crackles a distress signal he will experience a sense of recognition, a grasping of significance which the former, not open to that possible significance, simply cannot experience. Similarly a religious believer who looks on the world as a domain in which God may possibly manifest himself (in one way or another) has the potential for a whole range of significant experiences not open to the person without such a world-view. He does not just *view* the world in a religious way. He lives within it, and acts and responds and experiences its events and happenings (including his own feelings and states of mind) with the possibility in his mind that in doing so he may be coming in touch not just with the world and other people in it, but with the activity and manifestations of God.

We do not know, from a *sense* of recognition alone, or from what *feels like* discovering a meaning, that these are genuine sources of knowledge. (That, as we shall see, has to do with the reasonableness of the overall interpretative system.) But the experience raises that possibility, especially if we have other reasons for expecting significant events of the kind in question.

The religious world-view, then, not only brings out patterns (as Wisdom suggested) but gives possible significance to the patterns themselves, in a systematic, comprehensive way. And in doing so it triggers off further experiences, themselves open to interpretation within the system. All this is enough to put the believer in a quite different position from the non-believer, not merely as to his feelings, but as to additional experiences which for him are further relevant facts to be taken account of, in support of his belief about the reality of God.

It is the additional experiences resulting from or made possible by the world-view held, then, that are left out of consideration if we let the gardener story or duck-rabbit illustration define the situation. These include not only experiences of the mystical or 'immediate encounter' kinds, but also many of the experiences which were classed as *regenerative*, in chapter 1: the experiences of 'finding forgiveness for sins', 'being rightly guided', 'having one's prayers answered', 'being chastened by the Lord', and so on. These are not just religious ways of talking about ordinary experiences which anybody could have. For only under the religious interpretations do they have the profound personal significance and the subtle interconnections with an overall world-view and understanding of life which they have when experienced by the believer.

It is perfectly natural for the sceptic to say 'they are simply the ups and downs of life, and the feelings that go with them, read differently'. But isn't that just what is at issue, in the whole dispute about the truth of belief in God and the validity of religious experience? It is thus begging the question to agree from the start, as the duck-rabbit and 'experiencing-as' examples tempt us to do, that beneath the religiously interpreted experiences lie common facts which might just as well be experienced-as something quite non-religious.

It is perhaps recognition of those difficulties that has led Hick in a more recent book to rely less on the idea of experiencing-as and to begin his discussion of the rationality of religious belief by concentrating on the *distinctive* cases of religious experiences, the ones which Wisdom's gardener story and the duck-rabbit approach seem unable to cover.

WHY THE SOLIPSIST CAN'T HELP

The religious believer, it appears, draws support for his beliefs from experiences some of which the non-believer does not have. It may be out of the question then for the believer to present an argument from religious experience, since the premises themselves are not agreed upon. And of course, as most believers would insist, arguments on their own, without the relevant experiences, seldom convert people to religious belief.

But there is still the question whether the believer himself is reasonable in taking his experiences to support his beliefs. In other words, can a case be made for the rationality of beliefs based on religious experiences, even if an argument from them cannot be made so convincing that it will be irrational for a non-believer to reject it? This question Hick has put as follows:

> The question is not whether it is possible to prove, starting from zero, that God exists; the question is whether the religious man, given the distinctively religious form of human existence in which he participates, is properly entitled as a rational person to believe what he does believe.[11]

When do we regard people as rational? In matters of belief, the rational person is the one who holds his beliefs on adequate grounds (such as good evidence, sound inferences, or the reliable testimony of others). The grounds for a rational belief may vary from person to person. Consider, for instance, a belief about a past event, such as the Coronation Day of Queen Elizabeth II. Was it a fine day or did it rain? Some people will believe one thing (perhaps from old newspaper cuttings, or films they have seen). Others may agree, or disagree, on the basis of what someone who had been there told them. Others may have first-hand recollections of their own. Others again may be very cautious about trusting memories, and will not commit themselves until they have checked official weather records. 'How good is your evidence?' is the test for rational belief, and it can work in cases like that because we have agreed ways of deciding what kinds of evidence are to be relied on most, in reports about the weather.

Now people who hold religious beliefs on the strength of certain experiences believe themselves to have very good evidence, in some cases, even when it is the kind of evidence that cannot be easily shared, and for which there are no generally agreed standards of reliability. Does that mean there can be no answer to the question of whether or not they are rational, in believing as they do on the evidence they have? Well, asks Hick, have we any other cases where we treat beliefs as rational, even when no agreed body of solid evidence can be offered in support

---

[11] *Arguments for the Existence of God* (Macmillan 1970), p. 108.

of them? If we have, they might help us to know how to decide about the religious case.

To decide whether the believer's reliance on his religious experiences can be counted as a rational justification for his beliefs, Hick appeals to an argument used also in his earlier book *Faith and Knowledge*.[12] It can be called the argument from the reasonableness of not being a solipsist. A solipsist (*solus ipse*—'himself alone') is a person (largely invented by philosophers for the purpose of discussion) who believes that nothing at all exists other than his own experiences and states of mind. Almost all of us, almost all of the time, are *not* solipsists. We may have moments when we toy with the suggestion that there is really only 'the contents of my mind'. But we dismiss the thought and carry on as usual, treating the rest of the world as existing in its own right, communicating with other people, learning about how things were before we were born, and so on (none of which would make sense, if the solipsist view were right).

But what are our reasons for this anti-solipsist bias in our beliefs about reality? Why do we assume we are being more rational, in rejecting this possibility, than we would be in accepting it?

At first thought there would seem to be great practical advantages in *not* being a solipsist. After all, we might think, it must be a lonely state to be in. And how insubstantial everything must seem! But a convinced solipsist would have no difficulty in answering those objections. All the usual experiences of the company of other people, a real world, reliability, and so on would still be available. They just wouldn't reflect any reality beyond the experiencer's mind. But he need not even notice the difference. Everything could have its familiar 'feel' of reality; for after all, that is an experience too, and the solipsist is not denying any experiences, only realities beyond them.

There is then in the choice whether to reject or accept solipsism, Hick argues, an example of a situation in which we all consider ourselves rational in choosing one way rather than the other, and yet cannot *prove* that the way we choose is right. Can we even argue that it is the more rational of the two? Hick thinks we can, by attending to the character of our everyday experience, and to the way it affects us. Given the kind of life we lead and the kinds of experience we count as normal (rather than as

[12] Macmillan 1967.

84

dreams, madness, or hallucinations) we simply *cannot help* believing in the reality of an external world. And therefore, although no proof can be given one way or the other, it is more rational to believe that there *is* an external world, even though the alternative of solipsism is in theory always open to us.

Now, says Hick, transfer the argument to religious believers. And take as representative of them not the average, not-always-totally-convinced believer, but the outstanding religious personalities of history.

> If we consider the sense of living in the divine presence as this was expressed by, for example, Jesus of Nazareth, or by St Paul, St Francis, St Anselm or the great prophets of the Old Testament, we find that their 'awareness of God' was so vivid that he was as indubitable a factor in their experience as was their physical environment.[13]

They could not help believing in the reality of God behind their religious experiences (even though the possibility that they were deluded was, in theory, open to them). If we regard ourselves as reasonable in not being solipsists and in believing as we do in the reality of the external world, how can we deny that the great religious figures are also to be counted as reasonable (given their overwhelmingly convincing experiences) in rejecting the possibility of delusion, and believing as they did in the reality of God?

We should notice that this argument is different from the one considered above (chapter 3), where religious experience was compared with sense-experience. That was an attempt (not very successful, it was suggested) to show that the reality of the objects of religious belief could be found through religious experience in a way roughly parallel to that by which the reality of physical objects is known. In the present case, the parallel is being drawn not between two kinds of perception, but between two ways of justifying a belief, or showing it to be rational, in the absence of any proof or agreed criterion by which to settle the matter.

How good is the parallel? Hick admits that there are important differences between the possibility that we are mistaken in our sense of the reality of the external world, and the possibility that the great saints were mistaken in their sense of the reality

---

[13] *Arguments for the Existence of God*, p. 112.

of God. We are, after all, continually involved in experiences of the world, and cannot get away from it. Our environment forces itself upon us in a way that even for the most God-conscious believer God does not.

Again, believers in an external world are in an enormous majority, by comparison with doubters and solipsists. But then again believers in the reality of some sort of God are also in an enormous majority, at least amongst people who have the appropriate kinds of religious experience. It is not being argued that religious belief is reasonable for *everybody,* but that it is at least for those great religious figures who could not help but take their experiences as real. It then perhaps becomes reasonable for the ordinary rank-and-file believer as well, in that he has enough experiences in common with the great religious figures to justify his relying on their testimony in religious matters.

Has Hick succeeded, then, in showing that religious beliefs based on religious experiences can be counted as rational in certain cases? Most contemporary philosophers would agree with Basil Mitchell who, while sympathetic to Hick's intention, does not find the argument satisfactory. In his *Justification of Religious Belief* he considers Hick's discussion of the rationality of our familiar belief in a real world. There is no real question, he holds, about how we justify holding that belief rather than the solipsist position. 'It is not simply that we find ourselves under a psychological compulsion to believe in a world of things and persons; there is no coherent alternative.'[14] Solipsism, in other words, is not just difficult to believe in the face of our compelling sense of the reality of the world. It doesn't, in fact, really make sense. The would-be solipsist may say 'Perhaps my experiences are all that really exist'. But even in trying to state that position, he has to use words like 'my', 'experiences', 'what really exists', concepts which would be incoherent (they wouldn't hold together at all) if things really were the way he is trying to describe. (What would make experiences 'mine' rather than anyone else's?)[15]

If solipsism doesn't make sense, then it is not after all a possible alternative to our usual beliefs about the reality of the

[14] *The Justification of Religious Belief*, p. 109.
[15] The modern refutation of solipsism, in the work of the philosopher Ludwig Wittgenstein, is carefully explained in P. M. S. Hacker, *Insight and Illusion* (Clarendon Press 1972).

external world. And therefore we no longer have available the example of a reasonable-belief-held-without-a-rational-basis, on which Hick's argument depends. If the great religious figures are to be regarded as reasonable, then, in believing as they did on the strength of their experiences, a different kind of justification seems to be required.

WHETHER THE SAILOR REALLY SAW

What has led Hick (and Owen and others considered in the previous chapter) to rely so much on drawing a parallel between religious experience and perception of the real world has been the desire to take account of the *directness* religious experience has for the great saints and prophets. For them, Hick often reminds us, God was 'not an inferred entity but an experienced reality'. The same is no less true for the ordinary believer. 'He professes, not to have inferred that there is a God, but that God as a living being has entered into his own experience.'[16]

While we may agree with Hick that religious experience seems to those who have it to be more like a direct discovery than an inferred conclusion, we must consider now whether those two alternatives are as far apart from one another as he assumes. Hick himself recognizes that experience of God is not isolated from the other events and states of affairs in our experience, but rather seems to arise in and through them. There are special moments of worship and devotion. But there are also times when it is in the kindness of friends, the demands of one's duties, or the marvels of nature that one becomes aware of God's presence and activity.

Would the experiencing of God in that mediated way be better thought of as a discovery through interpretation, rather than as a perception of the divine reality itself? This is consistent with the view of interpretation as a kind of reading (see chapter 2) rather than a kind of perceiving. One reads the signs religiously and becomes aware of God through so reading them. The question whether one is reading them rightly is then a question neither about the validity of an argument, nor about the genuineness of a perception. It is a question about what possible justification there can be for the interpretative system (the way of reading) as a whole, so that experiences occurring under it and interpreted in terms of it can count as a reliable source of knowledge.

[16] *Faith and Knowledge*, p. 95.

A suggestion along those lines, as an alternative to the approach used by Hick, has been developed by Basil Mitchell. Mitchell's main thesis is that even though living religious experience is not a theoretical matter, showing that the beliefs based on it are able to be rationally justified *is*. The experiences in which believers find God seem to them to be instances of immediate awareness, not the conclusions of arguments. But that does not rule out the possibility that those experiences also need arguments to show them to be genuine. Nor does it mean that the occurrence of those experiences cannot provide support, in some theoretical and inferential way, to religious beliefs. Both acquaintance *and* inference, experience *and* reasoning, in other words, may have to play their part.

Mitchell provides an example to show that what is in fact an experience of reality may not be reasonably regarded as such without the aid of a good deal of argument and inference to back it up.[17] In a ship in stormy weather, the officer of the watch makes what he thinks is a visual sighting of a lighthouse. But because this fails to tally with the navigator's reckoning of the ship's position, it is concluded that the officer has made a mistake. Shortly afterwards, a lookout reports land on the starboard bow. The navigator is unconvinced, suggesting that it must be cloud. Then further cloud (or is it land?) appears on another bearing, consistent with the other sightings and further supporting the view that they *are* near land. Gradually opinion swings in favour of confirming that the officer of the watch really did see what he thought he saw.

The point of the story, Mitchell says, is this. Whether the officer was right in believing what he took to be the evidence of his own eyes can't be settled without some overall thinking about the situation. The navigator's reaction in suggesting that the officer had made a mistake seemed the more reasonable view at that stage. But as other reports came in, though all rather doubtful on their own, they added up to a convincing, cumulative case for treating the officer's apparent sighting as a genuine one. Even an instance of directly experienced reality then (the officer's original experience of seeing the lighthouse) may still need the support of a much larger body of reasoning before it can be counted as genuine knowledge.

Of course we know lighthouses are there to be seen. We are not so agreed about possible knowledge of God. Mitchell's

[17] *The Justification of Religious Belief*, p. 112f.

illustration is not intended to tell us anything about God. But it does tell us something about the contrast between knowing by experiencing and justifying that supposed knowledge by the use of wider reasoning. It shows that both direct experience and indirect reasoning may be required in our coming to know something, even by direct observation.

The example in fact makes a philosophical point about *knowledge*. Knowledge is systematic. Particular experiences, encounters with reality and the like, contribute to our knowledge (as do arguments and inferences). But they do so only when they can be systematically related to the other things we know. It is the interpretative system as a whole that must validate (if anything can) the experiences interpreted by it. As Mitchell says: 'The correctness of any particular interpretation cannot be guaranteed simply by the experience itself, but relies on a conceptual framework which draws support also from other, independent, evidence.'[18]

What, then, is the form of reasoning by which a whole religious interpretative system (a theology, if you like) can be justified, so that it is reasonable for those who experience things religiously in terms of that system to conclude that they are genuinely experiencing supernatural realities?

THE 'HOW ELSE DO YOU EXPLAIN IT?' ARGUMENT

The question of the rationality of religious belief-systems as a whole is much too big a topic to tackle here.[19] Our concern is with the part of religious experience in the wider argument (the 'cumulative case', as Mitchell has called it).

It was suggested earlier (end of chapter 4) that religious experiences give rational support to religious beliefs when they are the kinds of occurrence which would be *explained* if the

[18] *Ibid.*
[19] For recent discussions see Mitchell, *op. cit.*; Hick, *Faith and Knowledge*; T. Penelhum, *Problems of Religious Knowledge* Macmillan 1971); W. D. Hudson, *A Philosophical Approach to Religion* (Macmillan 1974); J. J. Shepherd, *Experience, Inference and God* (Macmillan 1975). Each of these treats the rationality of religious belief as a philosophical issue and attempts to take account also of traditional theological ideas of faith, revelation, and commitment. Many of the questions raised by religious belief are explored in *The Nature of Belief*, by Elizabeth Maclaren, in the Issues in Religious Studies series (Sheldon Press).

beliefs were true, and when no better ways of explaining them are available. This kind of reasoning can be described as the 'How else do you explain it?' argument. Its form consists of:

(i)   a general premise saying that if such-and-such is the case certain happenings will probably follow as consequences;
(ii) an observation that those happenings have taken place;
(iii) an assumption (or a further argument) that nothing else can account so well for those happenings;
(iv) a conclusion that therefore such-and-such *is* the case.

This is a form of reasoning we use all the time in everyday life. For example:

(a) If the cat has knocked over the milk bottle, milk will be spilt on the kitchen floor.
(b) Milk is spilt on the kitchen floor.
(c) The children have grown too old to knock over milk bottles, and nobody else has been near the kitchen.
(d) Therefore, it is highly likely that the cat did it.

Similar reasoning is regularly used in law-court proceedings, or detective stories, where conclusions are drawn from the evidence related to a crime.

(a) If the accused handled the weapon his fingerprints will probably be on it.
(b) Fingerprints like the accused's are on the weapon.
(c) It is highly unlikely that anyone else has the same finger-prints as the accused.
(d) Therefore, it is beyond reasonable doubt that the accused did handle the weapon.

There is nothing very difficult about that kind of reasoning in ordinary cases. Of course, we have to agree about the premises. (Somebody who doesn't agree that the children are too old to spill the milk, or that fingerprints are unique to each person, might be entitled to reject the conclusions.) But in usual situations we would have no difficulty in treating those arguments as thoroughly rational, even though they are not as rigorous as logical proofs or inferences from scientific laws.

We can now apply the same reasoning to religious experience and its possible evidential value in support of religious belief. The form of the argument goes as follows.

90

(a) If God (as described in belief-system S) exists, then experiences open to interpretation under S will be likely to occur. (For example, if S is Christianity, there are likely to be experiences of prophetic revelation, a holy or numinous presence, answered prayers, the sense of forgiveness after confession of sins, renewed lives following acts of faith, and so on.)
(b) Experiences interpreted under S do occur.
(c) No better ways of explaining the occurrence of those particular experiences are known.
(d) Therefore it is reasonable to conclude that God exists.

Unlike the premises of the earlier arguments, of course, many objections can be raised to each of (a), (b), and (c). The contentiousness of these premises and the enormous difficulty of knowing how to decide between competing views should not be allowed to obscure the fact that, underneath, the reasoning involved is really quite straightforward.

Meeting objections to those premises is a major task for the defender of any particular religious belief-system. Before trying to answer objections, however, people relying on the argument should be quite sure they understand the nature of the premises. Some further clarification is therefore called for.

(i) Premise (a) is largely a matter of being prepared to accept, for purposes of discussion, a certain theoretical account of what God is supposed to be like and what are the accepted signs of his activity in the world if he exists. As long as the theology or belief-system provides a description of what will *count as* the signs of the reality and activity of God, the only good reason for refusing to entertain the account as a logical possibility is if it is somehow incoherent. If the description contains contradictory ideas, of course, it cannot count as a premise, as it doesn't make sense to speak of either accepting it or not accepting it.

Deciding whether various concepts of God are coherent is a major question in philosophy of religion. The difficulty lies largely in the fact that much of the language used about God is metaphorical and oblique, and therefore it is not easy to say what is compatible with what.[20] (For instance, if God is said

[20] The philosophical problems related to language used in talking about God are discussed in my *Religious Language*, in the Issues in Religious Studies series (Sheldon Press).

to be 'absolutely good', and yet is also said to be 'the source of everything that exists', including all bad things, is there a contradiction?)

But let us assume for present purposes that a coherent concept of God can be stated, and with it is provided a good range of examples of what it means for God to act in history and human experience. That will be enough to clarify premise (a), and to make the argument one about whether such a God is likely to exist.

(ii) Premise (b) is uncontroversial in the case of some religious experiences where there is not much doubt that *something* public and inspectable has happened. Typical experiences of this sort would be cases of healings, prophecy, saintliness, speaking-in-tongues, feats of endurance, conversions, or prayers answered in recognizable ways. That such things do happen, however interpreted, is not in dispute. There will be much less agreement over experiences which are not so public (mystical illuminations, visions, the sense of God's presence) or which involve the occurrence of extraordinary and hard-to-confirm happenings (like levitations, materializations, and other paranormal phenomena).

(iii) Premise (c), however, is the most interesting one for our purposes. It asks the question 'How else do you explain it?' of religious experiences, and thus raises the subject of alternative explanations. The subject will be considered more closely in the next chapter.

But it is important first to make it clear just what it is about religious experiences that is to be explained. Of course what *causes* them is a crucial question, since the believer takes it that God is responsible for them, in some way or other (see chapter 6). But it is not only the occurrence of a religious experience that calls for explanation. It is also certain features of that experience; for instance, its compellingness, or the way it seems so relevant to the immediate needs and concerns of the person involved.

In particular, it is the apparently *systematic* character of typical religious experiences that explanations must be able to account for. By their 'systematic nature', I mean their relations with other experiences, actions, expectations, and beliefs. An interpretative system, as we have seen, gives a whole new range of possible meanings to experiences. Moral, emotional, intellectual, social, and personal aspects of experience are all integrated,

92

more or less successfully, into a theological system as a whole. Thus it is having-significance-within-a-system, and not just happening-to-occur, that is being referred to by the question 'How else do you explain it?'

But everyone knows, it may be objected, that absurd and mistaken belief-systems may still apparently work, in the sense that events occur which seem to fit them. And of course when such events are interpreted according to the systems, they produce the kinds of experience the systems envisage. (People who go looking for elves and fairies and really believe that they will find them will sooner or later come across *something* they think is strong evidence of their reality!)

No doubt there are such things as fruitful delusions and self-fulfilling beliefs. But even to suggest that is to agree that it makes sense to talk of belief-systems 'working out in experience'. And if that is so, then in explaining why belief in a certain system works, one possibility to be considered is that it works because the system is true (in whole or in part). And if that possibility is to be ruled out, a better alternative explanation must be given.

Anyone wishing to argue then that the apparently systematic nature of religious experience is simply an illusion, a web of fantasies and imagined connections, must do more than merely claim or suggest that it is. They must produce a better explanation, and not merely the hint of one, for discussion on its merits. That is why it isn't good enough for critics to say of religious experience that 'it's all a matter of your digestion' or 'it all depends on your upbringing'. Showing those explanations to be correct by producing the appropriate physiological or psychological laws is a very different matter from merely assuming that they are. But more of this in the next chapter.

The kind of reasoning that has been discussed in this section has a good deal in common with the testing and justifying of general theories in science. And in fact for the purposes of discussing its justification or rationality, a religious belief-system can virtually be treated as a theory or set of theories.

Religious believers, however, and especially theologians, are inclined to object strongly when such a suggestion is made. Belief in God is a matter of faith, not theory, they will insist. If religious belief is thought of as a hypothesis, doesn't that imply that it must be tentative, experimental, and ready to give ground in the face of contrary facts? Surely that is quite unlike the wholehearted commitment that goes with a genuine, living religious faith.

There's no doubt that commitment to one's beliefs is much more than a purely intellectual matter. How often do the pressures of daily life allow us to be completely rational and open-minded? We seldom have as much information to go on as we need. And none of us can reason perfectly, anyway. As a result we find ourselves having to act in quite unclear situations and to commit ourselves in ways we may be far from completely happy about in our minds.

That is especially so in matters of religion. Should we or shouldn't we join a protest march? Shall we have our children baptized? How shall we go about admitting to a 'religious persuasion'? After all, the moment we use any description of ourselves—'Jew', 'agnostic', 'Baptist', or whatever else—we shall be committed, whether we like it or not, and judged according to certain popular stereotypes.

So commitment beyond what is reasoned and justified is unavoidable in religion. And it may even be excusable on philosophical grounds. For might not a more or less committed, not-entirely-open position be in fact the best one from which to investigate and study religious experience at first hand? There may be no other situation in which one can develop those moral habits and sensitivities that the most convincing kinds of religious experience are often said to require.

For these and other reasons there is a great difference between looking on a belief-system as a theory or hypothesis, on the one hand, and living by a religious faith on the other. None the less, if the question being raised is the *rationality* of religious belief, then it *is* the intellectual aspects of the situation that count most. And then, what makes justifying religious beliefs rather like justifying scientific theories is not so much a matter of what religious belief is as of what *justification* is.

That is to say, when we are asking about justifying religious belief, or about the rationality of religious interpretations, we have no ready-made criterion of rationality in religious matters available to appeal to. Amongst the kinds of rational procedures we do have, the justification of comprehensive scientific theories (like the theories of gravity, natural selection, continental drift, and the like) seems to be the most promising for purposes of comparison.

If believers insist that belief in God is so unlike holding a scientific theory that we have no right to make the comparison, the cost of their doing so seems to be the admission that belief cannot, by any widely recognized criterion, be counted as rational. If on the other hand the way religious belief-systems are supported by an appeal to religious experiences *is* claimed as a rational procedure, the best way to show that is to bring out the parallels with reasoning used to support theories and hypotheses in the sciences, and with similar forms of reasoning used in everyday situations.

RELIGIOUS EXPERIENCE WITHIN A CUMULATIVE CASE

The approach suggested by Mitchell, of looking at a cumulative case in the justification of religious belief, has great advantages for taking account of religious experience in supporting belief. Unlike the models of intuition, encounter, or sense perception the cumulative case does not rest too much of its weight on the validity of any particular immediate experience taken to be of God (though it does not rule out the possibility that many such experiences are genuine). It takes the view that it becomes reasonable to believe they are genuine only when the system itself, under which they are so interpreted, is found to be rationally plausible. If knowledge or justified belief comes at all, then, it is by means of the total belief-system, not through particular experiences interpreted under that system on their own. Knowledge, as I have argued, is systematic.

Much of what theologians say about the importance (for a religion like Christianity) of the person-to-person nature of revelation, faith, and experience can be preserved, on this view. The sense of 'encounter', presence, or intuitive certainty many believers have does not *on its own* entitle them to claim direct awareness of God. But those experiences never in fact occur on their own. For they are experienced under a wider interpretative system, which may be able to bear far more weight than the individual experiences by themselves can. Once seen as linked with a theology which makes them 'the kinds of experience you might expect' if it were true, they are both supported by the wider belief system and in turn give it support within an overall, cumulative argument.

The cumulative case further allows us to take account of the great number of kinds of religious experience which do not fit at all well into the perceptual or immediate awareness models.

(For instance, experiences of changed lives, answered prayers, deliverance, and guidance in an individual's personal destiny or a nation's history.) It even allows religiously negative experiences, such as 'the sense of the *absence* of God', to have their part in contributing to the total fit between the concepts of the system (in that case, concepts such as judgement, sin, guilt, hardness of heart, and the like) and a range of human experiences and states of mind.

On theological grounds (i.e. in terms of the concepts of a system like Christianity itself) the cumulative case has obvious advantages. For if God exists and it is in fact true that 'in him we live and move and have our being' (Acts 17.28), there would seem to be no good reason for supposing that there can be only one or two possible ways of experiencing his reality. Too much reliance on any one model, then, whether that of revelation, perception, intuitive awareness, *or* inference from events and features of the world, would seem to be unjustified.

But it is from thinking about the nature of *interpretation* itself that the clearest support for the cumulative case approach can be found. Interpretation, as we saw, is a rational activity, by which particular events and experiences and states of affairs are found to have meanings in relation to one another and to wider experience, through their links with a belief-system. 'Meaning', 'significance', 'what the facts tell us'—these are not free-standing notions but systematic ones. Words have meanings only in languages. Signs (road-signs, for instance) signify only when they follow established regularities or conventions. Events make sense only when they fit into patterns, or make connections, or fulfil expectations. What religious belief-systems appear to do, then, is to make sense of experiences in a more comprehensive way than anything else.

A final point should be made about the use of the terms belief-systems and theologies. It is a mistake to take these terms in a static sense, as though the belief-systems of Christianity or any other religion are fixed and final, and all that is left is to find whether or not they seem to fit the experiences people are inclined to interpret in religious terms. For in fact theologies (like the religions they arise in) are constantly changing, more rapidly nowadays than even before, as alternatives are so much more widely known about. Knowledge of God through experience has always been regarded as a matter of learning, rather than an all-at-once affair. It seems reasonable to hold (with C. D.

96

Broad) that if there is truth amongst the belief-systems of religions, it is hardly likely to be all in one system, or in a final and complete form at any given time or place.

I have discussed the rationality of religious interpretations mainly by reference to the Christian theological system. But that does not mean that I have taken other possible systems to be incapable of defence on rational grounds. What I have tried to sketch in this chapter has been only a minimal position. It is an attempt to show some recent approaches to the question of rationality, and to suggest that the 'cumulative case' approach has the most to offer, in taking account of the many kinds of experience which people find relevant to their beliefs.

It is, on any account, an interesting fact that, given various existing religious belief-systems, experiences actually occur which lend themselves to being interpreted and related to one another in terms of those systems. I have suggested that where there are no better alternative explanations it is reasonable to suppose that the experiences in question support the credibility of the beliefs.

Clearly, ignorance of other possibilities is the chief reason why people commonly take it for granted that their familiar belief-system is the best. To what extent beliefs and systems of interpretation are able to stay alive and commend themselves to people who know of different kinds of experience and alternative ways of accounting for them is a very large question indeed. In particular, it has to do with the phenomenon of the persistence of religion in secular environments, and with the precedence one religion may take over another in a pluralistic culture.[21] Our final chapter will take those questions a little further.

[21] On the philosophical implications of 'the challenge of secularization' see W. D. Hudson, *A Philosophical Approach to Religion*, ch. 5.

6

EXPLAINING RELIGIOUS EXPERIENCE

> **CURSES REAL, SAYS PRIEST**
> A Maori Anglican priest said last night there were Maoris who had special powers to place curses on people and remove them. . . .
> Professor G. M. Vaughan, of the Auckland University psychology department, said it did not matter whether something was real scientifically. The important thing was whether someone believed it.
> 'If a young person believes that there are devils working inside them and that a *tohunga* [traditional Maori faith-healer] can get rid of them, it would be a valid treatment,' he said.
>
> Item in a New Zealand newspaper, November 1977

So the proof of the pudding is in the believing, is it? What really matters in the experiences religious people have—of demon-possession or mystical vision, faith-healing or conversion, answered prayer or the sense of God's presence—what really counts is that they *believe them to be* genuine religious experiences. That explains how they work. If you believe strongly enough that the experiences are real then they *are* real for you. What they may be for other people, or what they are in themselves, doesn't matter.

But is there more to be said than that? The psychologist who said the important thing is what someone believes was not necessarily contradicting the Anglican priest who thought there really was something in the *tohunga*'s powers. Obviously, if the powers don't work unless you believe in them, then believing in them is an important factor in their success. Yet that doesn't mean it is simply the believing, and nothing else, that makes the powers what they are. On that question, the psychologist does not commit himself. It is outside his province.

Yet the approach the psychologist takes seems very reasonable in the circumstances. 'Let's not argue about scientific explanations,' he says. 'What matters is how to treat a disturbed patient. If he believes the faith-healing powers of a *tohunga* can cure him, then that kind of treatment is valid for him.'

William James, as a psychologist, would have agreed with that pragmatic approach. In his *Varieties of Religious Experience* he firmly rejects the idea that the worth of an experience is to be decided by arguing over its origins (whether they are abnormal, natural or supernatural). It is fruits, not roots, that count most in our assessment of religious experience. Writing about conversions, for instance, he concludes, 'If the *fruits for life* of the state of conversion are good, we ought to idealize and venerate it, even though it be a piece of natural psychology . . .'[1]

Criticizing those who think they can debunk religious experiences by claiming they arise from mental or bodily disorders, adolescent personality-changes, and the like, James replies that the psychological and physiological roots of our states of mind have very little relevance to the values we place upon our thoughts and emotions.

ROOTS OR FRUITS?

It is often true that the best answer to the question 'Was so-and-so's experience a genuinely religious one?' seems to be, 'Wait and see; by its fruits we shall know it'. We saw in chapters 1 and 2 how religious experiences cannot be properly evaluated if they are detached from what comes before and after them—their total context of belief and life. The advantage of emphasizing fruits rather than roots is that it turns attention away from the 'feel' of the experience and takes account of its meaning within that wider context.

As James insists, we do not as ordinary people think it necessary to wait until we have a complete understanding of the chemical and psychological processes involved in our thoughts, perceptions, and experiences before we let ourselves (say) value tenderness more than anger, prefer ripe apples to sour ones, correct bad spelling, or decide whether to carry an umbrella. Such valuing and thinking can go on even when we are quite ignorant of the natural causal mechanisms involved in our

[1] James, *op. cit.*, p. 238.

99

brains. Explaining these is something we are quite happy, for all practical purposes, to leave to the scientific experts.

At least, that is so in the case of non-religious experiences. But with most religious experiences the interpretations involved commit the believer to certain views not just about their value, but also about their origins (i.e. what caused them, who is responsible for them). It is because of his belief that God (or some other non-natural agent in his belief-system) is involved in the occurrence and in some sense responsible for it, that the experience is able to have its characteristic effects on his life. His belief about the roots of the experience, in other words, seems necessary if it is to have those spiritual benefits for which he values it (i.e., its fruits).

This can be seen by considering cases where religious experiences lose their effects, once people alter their beliefs about what really causes them. Take familiar remarks like these:

> People stopped speaking of demon-possession when they came to understand more about medical disorders like epilepsy and hysteria.

> He gave up believing in God when he found that drugs could produce the same experiences as the saints and mystics had.

> Now we know that hallucinations can be caused through fasting and other changes in body chemistry, we can explain what people used to think were visions of angels or the Virgin Mary.

> What I took to be the filling of the Holy Spirit turned out to be merely a kind of trance-state in which automatic speech occurred.

> What the yogi thinks is intuitive awareness of ultimate reality is really just an altered state of consciousness which anybody can have, using bio-feedback equipment.

In all such cases, it is usual to say that religious experiences are being 'explained away'. The basis of each explanation is a change of opinion as to the roots, causes, or origins of the experiences.

Of course the fact that people give up beliefs in the light of fresh knowledge does not necessarily mean that their beliefs were false. Their reasons for giving up the beliefs may not be sound ones. C. D. Broad, for instance, argues strongly against our leaping to the conclusion that just because religious experiences are seen to have rather dubious psychological or physiological origins they cannot have anything like the exalted significance religious believers take them to have. In his argument from religious experience (discussed in chapter 3) he considers the objection that the great saints and founders of religions have commonly been abnormal people, eccentric, highly sensitive, and occasionally quite unbalanced. Doesn't that suggest that the experiences they had are likely to be delusory rather than genuine? Again, the religious experiences themselves often seem closely connected with other extremely unreliable states of mind —fixations and obsessions, irrational moods of joy or depression, neuroses, or powerful emotions like those of sex and fear. Is not this bad company which religious experiences keep enough to make us doubtful about their really having anything like the value religions have given them?

Broad is not unduly concerned. He reminds us that geniuses of all kinds have often been unbalanced. Sometimes this has helped them to be creative and imaginative. Sometimes it has been a result of the extraordinary discoveries they themselves have made, which took them far beyond the conventions and the usual assumptions of their contemporaries. There have been, he suggests, as many misfits and eccentrics among the forerunners of modern science as in the history of religion. So if the extraordinary things said and done over the years by many would-be scientists do not discredit the established findings of science, why should religion be differently regarded? We must allow the possibility, he says, that out of much delusion and misunderstanding in religious matters solid truths in time emerge and prove themselves to be fruitful and valid.

Broad thus excuses religion's seemingly disreputable roots, not on the grounds that they are completely irrelevant to its fruits but because they are just what one would expect, given the developing processes of history and human understanding. Such a view, however, is not likely to convince those who feel that far from a development, religion has suffered a decline, as scientific explanations appear to have taken away the meaning of more and more of what were once religion's most significant and corroborative experiences, and so made its established findings less and less relevant to modern life.

But there is another way to take account of fresh knowledge about the roots of religious experiences, more likely than

Broad's argument to appeal to modern religious believers. It is the argument that whatever emerges in the way of natural explanations, they cannot totally displace religious explanations. For the natural processes involved, whatever they are, may still simply be God's way of bringing about the experiences he intends people to have.

GOD AND NATURAL CAUSES

We saw in the previous chapter that the rationality of beliefs based on religious experiences depends in the end on there being no better explanations for them than those provided by the religious belief-system under which they arise.

Let us remind ourselves of the range of non-religious explanations of religious experiences that people nowadays can turn to. Conversions, with their sense of sin and guilt followed by forgiveness and new life, are explained as cases of a general behaviour pattern where emotional crises are followed by states of high suggestibility.[2] Ecstasy, hallucinations, hearing of voices, speaking in tongues, and the like are regarded as instances of abnormal behaviour with pathological mental and physical origins, close to those of delusions and insanity in general. Prophecy, inspiration, spirit-possession, charismatic leadership, revivals, and millenarian movements are explained sociologically, by reference to social and political conditions in which experiences of those types act as an outlet for the frustrations of repressed and deprived social groups.

Devotional habits and personal religious experiences are explained in terms of obsessive behaviour or wish-fulfilment, the projection of sub-conscious feelings on to an imagined object, or the mythological dramatization of the forces of nature. Other common religious experiences, such as answered prayers, a sense of God's presence, guidance, or providence, are explained in a common-sense way, as being largely a demonstration of 'the power of positive thinking'. And faith-healing, seership, and extraordinary physical abilities are pointed to as the kinds of things we can expect to be explained when the scientific investigation of ESP and paranormal phenomena is carried further.[3]

[2] See William Sargant, *The Mind Possessed* (Heinemann 1973).
[3] For articles on modern study of religion in anthropology, sociology, and psychology see 'Religion' in *International Encyclopaedia of the Social Sciences*, vol. 14 (Collier-Macmillan 1968).

Defenders of religious belief may react in two ways to such non-religious explanations of religious experiences.

(i) They may deny that the proposed natural explanations have been proved to explain genuine religious experiences.
(ii) They may insist that even if a complete natural explanation is given, it will simply be a description of 'God's way of doing things'.

Taken together, these responses seem a bit like the notorious defendant who tells the Judge: 'It wasn't me, your Honour. And anyway, I was acting in self-defence.' However there is more to (i) and (ii) than just an attempt to have it both ways.

(i) 'THE EXPLANATIONS AREN'T PROVED'

When the defender of religion makes this response, he is entering the dispute on the scientist's ground. If the supposed explanation is a psychological one, he must talk psychology. If it is a sociological one, he must engage in the kinds of reasoning and theorizing that go with the evaluation of sociological explanations and theories. And so on.

There are good reasons for thinking that many of the supposed non-religious explanations mentioned above are a long way from being proved adequate even in the terms of the sciences involved.[4] Thus if people wish to argue that religious explanations of various experiences have not been overruled by non-religious ones they are free to do so by showing that the latter fail, even on scientific grounds, to do the job properly.

Someone may argue that *any* non-religious explanations, however makeshift and stop-gap, will be preferable to the religious alternative. As Ninian Smart says:

> Of course, if one has already made up one's mind that the universe has no transcendent source and no transcendent side to it, that the only reality is the observable cosmos, then no doubt it will be easier to think that religion arises out of psychological and other urges. . . .'[5]

[4] For a thorough discussion of explanations of religious experience in terms of sociology, anthropology, Freudian theory, and the physiology of the brain see John Bowker, *The Sense of God* (Oxford 1973).

[3] *Philosophers and Religious Truth*, 2nd edn (SCM Press 1969), p. 124.

But that is simply jumping to a conclusion, not proving it scientifically.

And for that matter, isn't the religious believer who too readily relies on the view that natural explanations don't matter 'since God can work through them whatever they are' also doing a disservice to science? For he is opting out of the rational investigation of religion, an activity in which he, in particular, could usefully be involved because of his own familiarity with the subject. He is thus leaving the field open for less sympathetic and less well-informed researchers to set the standards.

Natural explanations of religious experiences, if they are fully to displace the religious explanations, must be able to account not only for the occurrence of the events and experiences, but also for their apparently systematic and purposeful nature. For the experiences, as we have seen, make sense in a wider context. They come as answers to prayer. They fit into patterns matching certain theological beliefs and meet certain doctrinal expectations. And occurring in the context of religious devotion and obedience, they seem to be more than just incidentally related to the situation and spiritual condition of the person who has them and to his other experiences. It is the apparent purposefulness and meaningfulness, and not their mere happening-to-occur, that needs to be taken account of.

The scientific investigator of religious experience may not be impressed by all that. Once it is admitted that some natural processes lie behind the experiences, he may be largely inclined to put the sense of purpose, special planning, consistency with theological criteria, and the like down to subjective and imaginary factors on the part of the person involved. ('All a matter of interpretation', it is commonly said.)

Alternatively he may seek to build into their natural causation an explanation of the apparent particular relevance and purposefulness of the experiences. Answered prayers, for instance, may involve auto-suggestion or even telepathy: the fact of people's praying in a certain manner helps to bring about the experience which is then regarded as an answer. Likewise, peace of mind following confession of sin and the reassuring words of a ritual of forgiveness may be just the sort of effect one would expect in the circumstances. There is no need to bring God into the story at all.

Of course the religious believer might at this point want to remind the scientist once again that his suggested explanations have yet to be conclusively proved. It is all very well to *say* that natural explanations can be given for all the apparently meaningful and suited-to-the-occasion features of some religious experience. It is another thing altogether to show, in a scientific way, how those explanations stand up to tests and counter-evidence. No one denies, for instance, that auto-suggestion exists. But is it to be simply assumed that a thorough study of prayer and the experiences which believers take to result from it would in the end confirm that auto-suggestion was the key to it all? Oughtn't the study to be done first, before a conclusion is reached?

Similarly with the other vaguely-described natural processes often thought to dispose of religious explanations of experiences (e.g. abnormal body-chemistry, neuroses, projected father-images, social deprivation, or wish-fulfilment). The verifying of such theories by rigorous, objective means has for the most part yet to take place.

Yet totally to ignore the scientist's attempts at explanation until they are fully substantiated does seem too defensive a position for a believer to take. It is likely to create the impression that he simply wants to keep religious experience in a special class bordering on the miraculous and permanently beyond natural understanding.

The believer may, however, have another reason for arguing that the natural explanations of religious experience cannot, *in principle,* be proved to be true. He may want to ask how we could ever *know* that a completely natural non-religious explanation of a religious experience had been given.

We have already seen how what is required is not simply an explanation of a similar experience interpreted non-religiously by someone else (see chapter 2). However alike some features of the situations might be, there are important differences in the experience itself when in the one case the experiencer interprets according to a set of religious beliefs, expectations, and associations and in the other he does not.

Suppose it were argued (as the believer often does argue) that in his case God chose to bring about a certain experience for a particular purpose—his conversion or regeneration, for instance, or the giving of a spiritual gift or mystical revelation. Even if a set of natural conditions sufficient regularly to cause that kind of experience in that kind of person on that kind of occasion were established (however that might be done) there would still be no way of knowing that the explanation given was in fact a completely natural, non-religious explanation. For the operating of natural causes in a case like that (i.e. a case where some such religious significance is involved) may, for all we know, require a further non-natural factor such as God's will which, though generally present in such cases, is not to be taken for granted as a constant law of nature. As W. J. Wainwright puts the point:

> Suppose we are presented with a causal account of religious experience which is believed by the scientific community to be fully adequate. Are we entitled to infer that the experiences are not genuine perceptions of God, etc? We are entitled to draw this conclusion . . . only if we have good reason to believe that the causes which are specified in that account can, when taken alone, i.e. in the absence of (among other things) any divine activity, produce the experiences in question. Without a disproof of the existence of God and other supra-empirical agents, it is totally unclear how we could ever know that this was the case.[6]

The point is, as Wainwright goes on to say, that scientific investigators cannot (so to speak) remove God from existence and show that those causes still produce these effects.

Does this entail that natural laws may hold at one moment, and not at another? If so, science would surely be impossible. Yet while it may seem very odd nowadays to suggest that laws of nature continue to hold only so long as God wills that they should (though traditional Christian theism says just that, in its doctrine of Creation) the oddness is perhaps because what we have in mind when we speak of natural laws are a relatively few very reliable general principles of the material world, like the laws of chemical reactions, of electricity and magnetism, or of the dynamics of solid bodies.

But the regularities, such as they are, according to which human thoughts and experiences occur may turn out to be very different from general physical laws—statistical rather than rigidly law-like, and allowing far less in the way of precise prediction. In their case, it might not be nearly so irrelevant or

[6] W. J. Wainwright, 'Natural Explanations and Religious Experience', *Ratio*, vol. xv, 1973, pp. 100–1.

superfluous to envisage God's will in some cases being a necessary factor and part-cause of the processes involved. As that possibility can never be excluded, it may be impossible to demonstrate that some purely scientific explanation, excluding all non-natural factors, has been found.

The notion of a complete natural explanation, then, is itself open to dispute and likely to be differently understood as between a religious and a non-religious scientist, even if both are committed to preserving the possibility of genuine science.

(ii) 'GOD WORKS THROUGH NATURAL CAUSES'

Theistic religions like Christianity teach not only that God is creator of the universe but also that even in the natural course of things within the universe, God's will is carried out (to some extent anyway— human beings commonly disobey him). There are, on this view, many purely natural processes which are carrying out God's will when they take place as they do. Not only are the sun, moon, and earth following their courses, producing day and night, winter and harvest, and so on, but also there are naturally-occurring phenomena making it possible for mankind to enjoy certain aesthetic experiences (bright flowers, pleasant-tasting foods, awe-inspiring storms, and so on), making human life good, according to God's will. And there are naturally-occurring human qualities, like sexual attraction, family love, courage and tenderness and generosity, which create and nurture human life and produce the kinds of things God desires for human beings.

Suppose, then, there also occur in the ordinary course of things (and thus open to investigation by physics, chemistry, psychology, and the rest) certain events and experiences which, interpreted within religious systems of thought and attitude, in various ways give rise to beliefs about God. They are taken to confirm his reality and to be evidence of his concern for the quality of human life. These experiences could all be the results of natural processes, yet at the same time achieve God's purposes for mankind, in arousing an awareness of his reality and an idea of his intentions.

Religious experiences, on that view, are identified not by some non-natural causation which alone can explain them, but by their religious significance: the beliefs and emotions they inspire, the thoughts they arouse about God, forgiveness, the life to

107

come, and so on, and the worship and behaviour they lead to. They are like signs built into nature, yet pointing beyond it.

A view along those lines has recently been stated by Maurice Wiles in *The Remaking of Christian Doctrine*. Speaking of experiences of God's purpose which play a vital part in man's experience of God, Wiles says,

> Particular events by virtue of their intrinsic character or the results to which they give rise give (like the beauty of the lilies) particular expression to some aspect of God's creative purpose for the world as a whole. They are occasions which arouse in us, either at the time or in retrospect, a sense of divine purpose. But that sense does not necessarily entail any special divine activity in those particular events. In so far as it is a genuinely religious sense of purpose to which they give rise, it is by pointing to a purposiveness within the world as a whole. Talk of God's activity is, then, to be understood as a way of speaking about those events within the natural order or within human history in which God's purpose finds clear expression or special opportunity.[7]

Similarly, it could be argued, with the naturally-arising ideas of God himself. Suppose it were shown that some of Freud's theories were valid and that it really was through an illusion, the unconscious projection of a father-figure, that people came to have their concept of a loving, all-powerful God. On this view, far from displacing God from the scene, the Freudian explanation could be taken as the very means by which God allows ideas of himself to arise in the minds of people for whom such a psychological process is the most suitable way to come to have religious ideas.[8]

Or suppose automatic speech, ecstatic trances, or charismatic prophecy in some cases led to social advances and religious or moral improvement. Then though they may come about by means which in other situations and with other effects would count as symptoms of mental disorder, yet in the religious cases they could be counted as the ways God works for the good of the people involved.

What are we to make of that suggestion? Is this how religious

[7] Wiles, *op. cit.*, p. 38.

[8] On psychoanalytic explanations of religious belief see section II of *Faith and the Philosophers*, ed. John Hick (Macmillan 1966).

experiences are finally to be accounted for? Wiles excludes the possibility that, in addition to being generally responsible for the world, God should also act in it as a part-cause of certain events and experiences.

> The experience of divine guidance or divine providence is so frequent and so fundamental to Christian experience that if it were to be understood as always implying special divine causation (however possible theoretically that may be), the occurrences of such special divine activity would have to be so numerous as to make nonsense of our normal understanding of the relative independence of causation within the world.[9]

Wiles is thus prepared to envisage the possibility of the human sciences becoming as successful at devising complete causal explanations of particular human experiences as the natural sciences are at explaining physical phenomena. That may seem highly unlikely, but, nevertheless, let us suppose that natural explanations could be found, not just in principle but in fact. On this argument if an experience, while arising naturally, produces a sense of God or in some other way furthers his purposes, then God is working through it. And that is so even if no non-natural factor at all is necessary for its causal explanation. The sense of *particular* involvement on God's part, his direct participation in the lives and destinies of the people involved, is simply an illusion—but a fruitful illusion, as it provides an occasion for affirming a *general* truth (about God's purpose for the world as a whole, his love for mankind, and so on).

An account of God's 'working through natural causes', along the lines Wiles suggests, could well take care of a good number of genuine religious experiences. It may in fact be true that for the average religious believer a large proportion of what are for him significant religious experiences are simply naturally-occurring occasions (including occasions brought about by the actions of other people) on which he experiences with fresh conviction and clarity what he believes to be general truths about God's creation of and purposes for the universe.

But then the question arises, where does the knowledge come from, that God's overall purposes for the universe are such-

[9] Wiles, *op. cit.*, pp. 37–8.

and-such? If, as is usually thought, it is a conclusion reached from treating certain historical events and experiences as especially defining God's character and will, then there would need to be something about *those* experiences which made them more indicative of God's character and purposes than any other possible experiences (even if, as the Creator of nature, God were in a sense responsible for all experiences whatsoever).

Not every religious experience, in other words, can be just a reminder of general truths about God. Some must also be sources of, and instances of, those truths. Otherwise what would the content of those truths be, and where would mankind obtain knowledge of them?

The God-is-working-through-it-all position, then, fails to do justice to the key experiences of the founders and great figures of religious traditions, and also the high points in the lives of believers which they take to be particular experiences of God as *active and present to them in particular*. The 'sense of encounter with God' is, as we have seen (chapters 4 and 5), by no means infallible, but in its most characteristic forms, whatever the natural medium involved, it has been taken to be a particular occurrence for which God is in a special way responsible.

There is, then, a logical point to be considered. Unless it is open to us to believe that God has actively brought about some and not others of the experiences religions take as defining his character and purposes, we lack any basis for crediting him with one set of purposes rather than any other. If *all* natural events and experiences are equally the work of God, there is no reason for saying that the sense of God's character and will aroused by one set of experiences is a revelation of God, while excluding the quite different conceptions of God (for instance, as malevolent, wasteful, or unconcerned) which might be brought to mind by paying attention to a different set of experiences.

How then is it possible to preserve the specialness of the events and experiences which are supposed to be the most significant in a religious belief-system, the points at which God's purposes and action are revealed? One way, of course, is to treat them as miraculous events (in a strict sense of miracle—not just a watered-down sense like 'wondrous happenings which make us think of God'). In that case, there would be no question of the religious explanation competing with the scientific explanation. For a miracle is an occasion on which the usual regularities of nature are upset and cannot therefore be explained by scientific means.

For some people, the idea of treating all the really significant religious experiences as miracles would be an ideal way of guaranteeing them the importance, and immunity from scientific explaining-away, they might wish them to have. A miracle would then occur whenever a genuine religious conversion took place, a prayer was answered, or an experience occurred bringing spiritual enrichment, a sense of the divine presence, or a moment of numinous awe or mystical rapture. Other religious people find it very difficult to use the concept of contrary-to-nature miracles in so widespread a way. For they are aware of the unwelcome consequences of allowing miracle-explanations to take the place of scientific investigation.

There are many miracles claimed by many religions. Most believers want to claim their own religion's miracles, or some of them, as genuine, but not to allow that those of the other religions (or of groups within their own tradition of which they disapprove) are also genuine. And if they are to deny them, then some sort of natural explaining-away of the other miracles is necessary. (For instance, Protestants often simply take it for granted that the tales of wonders worked by Catholic saints are legends with little foundation in fact.)

But having admitted that what look like other miracles (but in their view aren't) must have natural explanations, they can hardly deny that the same reasoning might be applied to their miracles too. In other words, the consideration of possible natural explanations of religious experiences is every bit as important for those who rely on the notion of miracles as for those who don't.

For the scientist, the concept of miracles poses a serious professional problem, a problem about the discipline of science itself. A scientist may believe in God, and even believe that miracles are possible in principle. But to be a consistent scientist he must proceed on the assumption that adequate natural explanations can in time be found for all events that occur within nature. Finding those explanations is what science is about, and it has been able to succeed as it has done, only where the possibility of miraculous, contrary-to-nature explanations has been systematically excluded. For once miraculous explanations are envisaged, we can never be sure that we are not shutting the door prematurely on a natural explanation being found in due course.

Thus while a religious believer who is a scientist might be prepared to treat a few crucial religious events as miracles (the miracles of Jesus and the apostles, perhaps, and the resurrection—though his uncommitted colleague looking on, or a believer from another religion, might find that particular choice of miracles rather arbitrary and subjective) he could hardly feel at all happy, as a scientist, to see the whole range of religious experiences (healings, visions, answered prayers, conversions, saintliness, and so on) all put into the category of miraculous disturbances of the order of nature. He is far more likely to view them as instances where God works in and through nature, rather than contradicting it.

The notion of miracle, then, seems to require very sparing use, if it is not going to destroy the scientific enterprise (which, for the religious scientist, is itself one of God's gifts to humanity).

There is, however, another way in which it can be argued that God works both generally and in particular through natural processes, a way which keeps close to traditional views, yet avoids the conflict with science which talk about miracles produces. This is the view that there are enough purely chance factors within nature for there to be ample scope for God to initiate certain events and experiences, without miraculous interventions to suspend any natural laws.

In a paper called 'Praying for Things to Happen' Peter Geach has pointed out that in ordinary affairs we simply take for granted without question a fair number of chance occurrences within nature, and indeed our freedom to act and choose depends on there being such openness about the way things go.[10] Yet as the Book of Proverbs says, Geach reminds us, even chance events may not fall outside God's purposes. 'The lot is cast into the lap; but the whole disposing thereof is of the Lord's (Proverbs 16.33).

If this is met with the reply that behind the apparent chance occurrence of some events, all events in the material world are in fact really determined in their causes and predictable in principle if only we knew the physical forces involved, Geach's answer is that such a view rests merely on 'a superstitious belief in the predictive feats of science'. It has not been established, either as a necessary truth or as a conclusion proved by the

[16] In *God and the Soul* (Routledge & Kegan Paul 1969).

112

findings of empirical research. A physicist, he says, 'cannot predict how dice will fall any better than I can'. For in fact the more accurate the information a physicist is given about the forces acting on particular dice, the more precise prediction becomes impossible, owing to the ultimate unpredictability of sub-atomic particles.[11]

If there *are* chance events in nature (as we take for granted, whenever we weigh up probabilities) then the idea of God's acting within the world through natural processes, yet not in conflict with natural laws, cannot be ruled out. If it could be shown, for instance, that chance events are a feature of human brain processes, that finding could be very relevant to the beliefs of most religions (especially the biblical one) that God or other supernatural beings can influence a person's thoughts, dreams, and emotions. The same may be true in the public area of history and society, where again large-scale events may result from what in natural terms contain chance factors whose outcome one way or another could not have been predicted, and therefore whose complete explanation falls outside the scope of science. Furthermore, the enormous role of chance events in genetic variation is becoming an accepted fact of modern biological and evolutionary theory.[12]

Of course, even if God were to act within nature, through being responsible for chance events turning out so as to lead to certain experiences, the achievement of that end would depend on the usual natural processes (whether physical, psychological, or social) for the most part following their regular paths. So allowing the possibility of divine action of that kind would not upset the general effectiveness of science as a source of reliable knowledge about the world.[13]

The question whether religious experience can survive the scientific study of its natural mechanisms is part of the wider question of how much human experience as a whole can retain its customary meanings and values, as knowledge increases about the workings of people's minds and brains. It seems impossible for us to state a general rule about how far scientific explanations

[11] On indeterminism in nature see J. R. Lucas, *The Freedom of the Will* (Oxford 1970).

[12] See Jacques Monod, *Chance and Necessity* (Fontana edn 1974).

[13] On the moral and theological questions raised by the idea of particular divine action in the world, see Brian Hebblethwaite, *Evil, Suffering and Religion* (Sheldon 1976).

of human behaviour affect our beliefs about human actions, emotions, and intentions. So is it really surprising that no general rule can easily be found to cover the case of events and experiences for which God is supposed to be responsible?

The same is true of the question often asked about the value of drug-induced and other forms of artificially-aroused states of consciousness. They are like such things as hypnotically-influenced sports achievements, genetically-engineered species, organ-transplant operations, or artificially-inseminated conceptions. When people ask 'Are these things genuine, valid—to be encouraged or frowned upon?' the simplest answer is that we don't know yet, because we haven't decided. For it is up to us to a large extent to *discover* how to evaluate such things, as we find whether or not they can be satisfactorily accepted into the fabric of our constantly-developing cultural and religious traditions.[14]

WHETHER RELIGION IS SUPERFLUOUS

In this chapter we have considered the suggestion that whatever natural processes may be found to lie behind religious experiences, it is still open to the believer in God to say that natural explanations are only a part of the story that must be told, if the full meaning of the experience is to be grasped. For the believer, of course, what religious explanations take care of (and what purely natural explanations leave out) is the systematic, interrelated character of his experiences. They seem to him to be part of a wider scheme of things.

Thus in the course of a person's life he may have occasional mystical states of mind (possibly a biochemical imbalance in the brain), go through a conversion (familiar enough, especially during adolescence), be impressed by a relative's recovery after faith-healing (could have been hypnosis), lose his job through redundancy and suffer a period of deep despair and solitude (a case of depression), be brought back to health through the encouragement of a friend (everyone needs a friend), providentially find a new career after much prayer and patient trust in God (well, the economy was improving), and come to

[11] For a difficult but important discussion of experience-inducing drugs and claims about religious experiences, see Bowker, *The Sense of God*, ch. 7.

have great peace and a sense of ultimate purpose in his everyday experiences (a comfortable illusion).

In each case, a perfectly ordinary, non-religious explanation can be given. But according to those explanations his experiences have no intentional connection with one another, or with the overall course of his life. They are simply natural processes which happen to occur to him as and when they do.

The religious explanation, on the other hand, treats the experiences not just one by one. but as part of a pattern. It offers a comprehensive world-view, linking a personal life-story with similar experiences of countless other people and with the ideas and concepts of whole traditions of thought and belief. Through religion the meaningfulness of one person's experiences is related in the end to purposes embracing the whole cosmos and human life within it.

It is the enormous integrating power religious interpretations have, then, that keeps religion alive even when natural explanations are also available. The purpose and order found in experience relevant to one's own personal destiny and recognized in the lives and destinies of others is accounted for under the religious explanation and not in any other way. For religious belief-systems are uniquely able to link the natural, scientific understanding of things with the personal, moral, and imaginative aspects of human life. So long as people continue to look for that kind of total, all-embracing explanation for their experience, they will consider that religion has more to offer them than science, for it is by far the more comprehensive of the two.[15]

In this book we have considered mostly the *positive* religious experiences—those that reflect the discovery of God and the enjoyment of the benefits of religious faith. But it must not be assumed that religious experiences are largely of a comfortable, reassuring kind, most suitable for those who are reluctant to face the realities of life. For religion thrives as much on grim realities as on sweetness and light.

For most of mankind life involves tremendous frustration and suffering, and much pointless horror and sadness. Yet from a religious point of view pointlessness, terror, and disaster themselves seem to stand out against a background of what could have been or what ought to be. The whole order of things, it is felt, has broken down, wherever human life is stifled and

[15] See Don Cupitt, *The Worlds of Science and Religion* (Sheldon 1976).

115

hopes are unfulfilled. Despair at this disorder is one of the very things that has always led to thoughts of God.

When confronted with the horrors of cruelty, war, famine, and disaster, men and women still react with a religious sense of outrage. Such things are felt to be tragic and wrong, not just ordinary and natural. Loss, suffering, and disharmony themselves become religious experiences, and purely scientific, non-religious explanations of them (for all their practical usefulness) leave out whole dimensions of depth and meaning.

These dimensions seem to be captured only by speaking of things like cosmic evil and human corruption, sin, guilt, and spiritual disorder. And the answers to the questions they pose seem to be found only by appealing to ideas like God, enlightenment, salvation, grace, and the supreme religious values of faith, hope and love. So people who go on making religious interpretations, even when they are quite aware of the natural factors involved, are not being inconsistent or irresponsible. They see it as a way of trying to be true to their own experience, and to what they know to be the experiences of the human race.

BIBLIOGRAPHY

Baelz, P. R., *Prayer and Providence*. S.C.M. Press 1968.

Bowker, John, *The Sense of God*. Clarendon Press 1973.

Hepburn, R. W., 'Religious Experience', in *Encyclopaedia of Philosophy*, ed. Paul Edwards, vol. 7. Collier-Macmillan 1967.

Hick, John, *Arguments for the Existence of God*. Macmillan 1970.

Hick, John, ed., *Faith and the Philosophers*. Macmillan 1966.

James, William, *The Varieties of Religious Experience*. Fontana 1960.

Katz, Steven, ed., *Mysticism and Philosophical Analysis*. Sheldon Press 1978.

Lewis, H. D., *Our Experience of God*. Fontana 1970.

Miles, T. R., *Religious Experience*. Macmillan 1972.

Owen, H. P., *The Christian Knowledge of God*. Athlone Press 1969.

Smart, Ninian, *The Religious Experience of Mankind*. Fontana 1971.

Smith, John E., *Experience and God*. Oxford University Press 1968.

Studies in Religious Experience, published by the Religious Experience Research Unit, Oxford (Edward Robinson, *The Original Vision*; Timothy Beardsworth, *A Sense of Presence*; Edward Robinson, ed., *This Time-Bound Ladder*, R.E.R.U. 1977).

Thouless, R. H., *An Introduction to the Psychology of Religion*, 3rd edn. Cambridge University Press 1971.

Zaehner, R. C., *Mysticism, Sacred and Profane*. Clarendon Press 1957.

Other books in the Sheldon Press Issues in Religious Studies series particularly relevant to religious experience are *The Nature of Belief*, by Elizabeth Maclaren, *Religious Language*, by Peter Donovan, and *Evil, Suffering, and Religion*, by Brian Hebblethwaite.

INDEX